© Naumann & Göbel Verlagsgesellschaft mbH, a subsidiary of
VEMAG Verlags- und Medien Aktiengesellschaft, Cologne
www.vemag-medien.de

Cover Photography: Uwe Ziss, Düsseldorf
Design: WirtzCologne

Complete production: Naumann & Göbel Verlagsgesellschaft mbH, Cologne
Printed in Slovenia
07/39
ISBN 978-3-625-11173-3

Wok

Contents

Ingredients

The worldwide success of cooking with a wok is based on a convincingly simple concept: fresh ingredients, short cooking times and aromatic spices. Whether vegetarian, poultry, meat, fish or seafood — uncomplicated and delicious dishes can be created within minutes using a wok. We would like to introduce you to this fascinating piece of equipment that has become the epitome of healthy cooking.

Cooking with a Wok

Cooking with a wok is more than just a glimpse of a different way of cooking – it's an excursion into Asian culture. The history of the wok goes back to China, as many as 3,000 years ago. The pot (or 'wok' in Cantonese) came to exist out of a need to prepare food quickly using only a single source of fire. The invention proved to be highly versatile and economical, resulting in the huge popularity of the wok all over Asia and lately even Europe.

We would like to introduce you to this gastronomic culture with a history of thousands of years. It is based on an attitude to food as being more than a mere necessity, but a vital means of achieving a harmony of body, mind and spirit. The principles of Asian cuisine are extremely simple: A person should feel well after eating. This is only possible with balanced nutrition, i.e. the ingredients need to fulfil special basic requirements. These include:
- fresh food of the season
- short cooking times
- aromatic spices

Asian cooking utensils match the perfection of the Asian art of cooking. Let's start with the wok, this large round-bottomed pan. The timeless design is made of a practical material and requires relatively little energy. The latter was particularly significant in ancient China, because firewood was scarce.

Since Asian cooking has become fashionable, woks made of all sorts of materials have become available in various shapes and sizes.

If you are considering buying a wok, make sure that you choose a design that suits you. There are woks with two handles or with a single long handle. Both are equally good to work with.

The additionally available accessories are intended to make cooking and preparing Asian food easier. Most woks are sold as sets.

Any further utensils that you may need are available in Asian food stores or in many other appropriately stocked shops.

Metal rack

A generally semicircular metal rack is a basic wok accessory. It is attached to the upper edge of the wok to allow finished fried food to drain while keeping it warm at the same time.

Lid

A lid is also part of basic wok equipment. Usually made of stainless steel, aluminum or heat-resistant glass, it is mainly used for steaming.

Spatula

The wok spatula looks like a small shovel with raised outer edges. The front edge of the metal blade is slightly rounded to allow smooth stirring and lifting of food in the wok. The handle of the spatula is relatively long and made of wood or plastic.

Skimmer and bamboo sieve

There are two types of sieves: The skimmer, a wire mesh which can be fine or wide with a bamboo or wooden handle, is used for lifting deep-fried food out of the oil or for moving the portions around in the hot oil to achieve even browning. There are also bamboo sieves in various sizes with or without draining dishes or smaller wire sieves with long handles or handles made of bamboo.

Cooking chopsticks

Real professionals use cooking chopsticks for stirring food in the wok. These are longer than the chopsticks used for eating, to allow access to the bottom of the wok without any danger of burning the fingers.

Bamboo tongs

Bits of finished food can be taken out of the wok easily using bamboo tongs. The tongs are particularly useful for those who have yet to master the art of using chopsticks.

Wok brush

The brush is another useful and traditional multifunctional wok accessory. It is used to stir fry very finely chopped ingredients, the fine ends of the whisk being better suited for this purpose than the large spatula. The brush is also used for cleaning the wok under hot running water. The brush is made of cut bamboo fiber and should never be cleaned with detergent. It should simply be allowed to dry naturally after rinsing thoroughly.

Steamer basket

Steaming vegetables and fish is the most common cooking method in China. The various sizes of bamboo baskets used are covered and placed in a wok filled with boiling water. The rising steam passes through the basket without any water actually coming in contact with the food. The steam-

ing baskets are not only functional but also attractive, and are therefore also frequently used for serving the food.

Chopping knife

Those fearless enough to use authentic equipment should acquire an Asian kitchen chopper with chopping board. This type of chopping knife is used for all sorts of things in Asian cooking. In addition to fine and coarse chopping, it is also useful for filleting, grinding and tenderizing meat. Asian cooks generally own three types of chopping knifes that vary according to weight and purpose.

Chopping board

A good chopping knife needs a solid chopping board to go with it. Round slices of hardwood cut out of tree trunks in one piece are valued for Asian cooking. The blocks and boards made out of laminated rods or layers of wood generally available are ideal for this purpose.

Cooking and Preparation

In Asian cooking, great importance is attached to the preservation of the color, structure, fragrance and taste of food. This requires a harmonious and balanced selection of individual ingredients. These extensive preparations take up considerably more time than the cooking itself. Chopping the ingredients is a way of keeping cooking times short.

It also makes sense to cut the ingredients requiring less cooking time into larger morsels than those that need to be cooked longer. Ingredients with different cooking times can also be blanched or cooked in advance to make sure that the whole meal is done at the same time. Various herbs and spices should be fried to flavor the oil for the next ingredients.

Cooking methods

Stir-frying

Stir-frying is the most popular and well-known method of preparing food in a wok. The ingredients are heated in very little, but very hot oil, and continuously moved around in the process. This allows them to be cooked within minutes, without the loss of any natural flavor, vitamins and nutrients. Meat becomes very crispy outside, while remaining wonderfully succulent inside. Vegetables stay crisp and crunchy. Since stir-frying is such a fast way of cooking, previous preparation of the ingredients is vital.

Braising

Braising involves frying smaller quantities of the ingredients in the wok first and then adding liquid (water, seasoned stock etc) and stewing them while covered with a lid. This method of cooking is particularly suitable for the preparation of coarse-fiber meat. Red cooking is a typically Chinese cooking method. The name is derived from the large proportion of dark liquids, such as for example soy sauce, in which the dishes are braised after being fried briefly.

Deep-frying

Deep-frying involves frying the ingredients — raw or wrapped in some type of batter or pastry - in hot oil. Deep-frying in a wok does not require anywhere near the quantity of oil required for other deep-frying methods. It is important to make sure that the oil has the right temperature, i.e. that it is hot enough. To find out if this is the case, immerse a wooden chopstick in the oil. If small bubbles are formed on it, you can start deep-frying.

Steaming

Steaming is a classical cooking method in China. The ingredients are put into water-soaked steamer baskets, which are placed in a wok containing a little liquid and then steamed until cooked. It is important that the steaming basket and the food to be cooked do not come in contact with the liquid in the wok while steaming and that the wok is closed properly during the steaming process.

Cooking/Boiling

The wok's reputation as a multi-purpose utensil is justified. It can naturally also be used for more basic cooking and boiling. Soups and stews can be prepared in a wok by first frying the ingredients briefly, then adding liquid and allowing the mixture to simmer for some time. More elaborate, but certainly interesting and worthwhile, is the method of preparing meat in the wok by first boiling and then frying it. This leaves the meat with a very tender inner core combined with an outer crispiness.

Baking/Frying

The wok is an all-round talent, and can of course be used for baking in the sense of frying. The traditional wok has a hemispherical shape, with a curved bottom. The bases of European wok varieties are generally flattened, however, to make it easier to use them on the commonly electric cooking stoves. Small pancakes, dough for spring rolls and small stuffed pastries, such as e.g. rotis, are baked — with a savory filling — by frying or deep-frying in hot oil.

Vegetables in a Wok

Vegetables and woks are made for each other. Vegetables can be cooked within minutes in a wok, without losing any of the natural flavor, vitamins and nutrients. The vegetables keep their crunchy texture and taste, thereby fulfilling a basic requirement of Asian cuisine: freshness and simplicity.

Asian cooking includes some exotic vegetables that are essential for making vegetable dishes cooked in a wok so attractive. White egg plant from Thailand, pak choi from China, a mustard cabbage with a mild aroma reminiscent of Chinese cabbage (sometimes also spelled bok choy). Okra (also known as lady's fingers) are the longish, unripe fruits of the okra plant, while water chestnuts are the dark brown bulbous fruits of a water plant that has nothing in common with nuts except that water chestnuts also have to be peeled. Bitter cucumbers and yard-long beans on the other hand, are similar to the familiar European vegetable varieties. Yard-long beans are about 12 in/30 cm long and are excellent for cooking in a wok. They can be replaced by green beans if need be. The exotic lotus root is available either fresh or pickled.

Asian mushroom varieties such as oyster, straw, shiitake, mu-er or nameko mushrooms are a must for wok cooking. Straw mushrooms are Chinese cultured mushrooms with a delicate flavor. They have a spherical shape, with a gray-black color and cream-colored lamellae. The shiitake mushroom on the other hand, is a very tasty tree fungus used for flavoring many dishes and said to possess healing powers in Asian countries. Because of their shape, mu-er mushrooms are also known as cloud ear mushrooms. The nameko mushroom is a kind of pholiota mushroom. All of the mushroom varieties are not always available fresh, but certainly dried.

Vegetables can be cut into pieces, slices or strips, as desired. Particularly hard vegetables, such as carrots,

cucumbers, celery or radish can be cut into even slices using a vegetable grater. Very thin slices can also be obtained using a peeler. Greens should be cut into wider strips of about 1 ¼ in/3 cm because of their fast cooking time. There are no boundaries for individual imagination in this respect. Cutting vegetables in strips or slicing them diagonally is very decorative.

Rice – a Gift of the Gods

For Asians, eating rice is the quintessence of eating. A meal without rice is virtually unthinkable. There has to be something very special about this oldest cultivated plant that made it the staple food of almost half of the world's population. Rice ideally complements the well-seasoned Asian meat, fish and vegetable dishes.

Expressed by the flowery language of the East: ' ... rice accompanies the other dishes into the stomach in a pleasant manner...' More attention has also been paid to rice in Europe for some time now. It has been realized how many vital substances are packed into the tiny grains: vitamins, minerals, carbohydrates, trace elements, dietary fiber and lots of high quality, easily digestible protein. The preparation of rice is both quick and varied, leaving the eater feeling pleasantly full, without making the stomach feel heavy. The approximately 8,000 different types of rice can be divided into three different shapes: long, medium and short grain.

Long grain rice is characterized, as the name implies, by long, narrow, relatively hard grains. These keep their grainy texture after cooking. The most well known type is patna rice, available commercially as natural and parboiled rice. The latter retains the nutrients that are normally lost by the processes of refinement such as grinding and polishing, by means of a special procedure. A wonderful Asian delicacy is basmati rice: a specialty that makes you look forward to eating before the rice is even finished because of the lovely smell developed during cooking! Medium and short grain rice not only look different than long grain rice, but also have a softer internal structure. White short grain rice is the most common variety of rice in all parts of Asia where chopsticks are used for eating. The reasons are obvious: although the individual grains are dry and loose after cooking, they stick together a little, just enough to allow them to be eaten with chopsticks. Cooking rice is actually not as difficult as it may seem. We use the Chinese way of cooking rice, which works every time and is as follows: Two cups of dry rice are placed in a pot. Three cups of water are poured over the rice. Add salt to taste. Bring the mixture to the boil and then continue to cook at a low temperature until the rice has absorbed all of the water. This makes five cups of boiled rice.

For Japanese people, rice is more than just a staple food — it symbolizes food as well as culture. The grains were once so precious that the possession of 'white gold' was the ultimate measure of wealth. Even the belligerent Samurai accepted freshly harvested rice as payment. Even today, people who have moved from the countryside to the city have a small sack of freshly harvested rice sent from their old home. Fresh rice has a very intensive taste of earth, air, sun and water, and should on no account be spoiled by additions that would detract from this special taste. It may be difficult for Europeans to understand this kind of Japanese logic in this respect, since we generally consider rice only to be a more or less essential filler that tastes quite nice.

Noodles – a Serving of Good Luck

Noodles promote long life and happiness according to an ancient Chinese saying familiar all over Asia. The huge diversity of noodles available is therefore not surprising. Noodles form the basis of a whole range of dishes and also provide plenty of variety as far as appearance is concerned. Noodles are just as popular in Asian cuisine as rice. They even constitute the staple food in some regions. Noodles did not, however, manage to completely replace rice even in the noodle-dominated areas, with some noodle varieties being in fact made of rice flour.

Glass noodles, for instance, are made of soybean flour and stay transparent even after soaking. Hot water is poured over them and they are allowed to swell up for some time, but not boil. All the other ingredients can be cooked in the meantime, with the well-drained noodles finally being added by folding them in gently. The neutral taste of these noodles makes them a perfect counterpart for all sorts of spices.

Rice noodles are dried, almost transparent and, in contrast to glass noodles, turn snow-white after soaking. As indi-cated by the name, these noodles are made of rice flour and have a similarly delicate rice flavor. Rice noodles are available in various widths, from very thin sticks to wide ribbon noodles. Deep-frying them quickly while dry makes them look particularly decorative.

Egg noodles, which are most similar to European noodles, are also important, particularly for Thai cooking. The only difference is the type of eggs used: goose or duck eggs are used instead of chicken eggs in Thailand.

These very ordinary ingredients can also be enriched with a special kind of fragrance by adding a hint of a flavor of dried prawns or seaweed.

Both egg and wheat flour noodles are available in a great variety of sizes and widths in Asian food stores. Noodles are often pre-cooked, so that they only need to be soaked or briefly covered with boiling water.

Fresh noodles may be available in some particularly well-stocked Asian food stores. This is a culinary highlight that should not be missed.

Meat and Poultry in a Wok

Wok-fried meat and poultry is crispy brown and crunchy outside while remaining succulent and tender inside. Using only little oil at high temperatures, there is no healthier and faster way of cooking meat and poultry. The actual cooking time in the wok is very short, so the meat and poultry needs to be prepared beforehand. Beef and pork is best cut into thin strips, while lamb is normally cubed. Chicken or duck are also cut into thin strips.

Standard procedure is to first fry the meat in little, but very hot, vegetable oil for a short time, the different types of meat requiring different cooking times. Lean chicken is done faster than beef or pork for instance. The meat is moved and turned around all the time while frying. It is finished after a few minutes and can be taken out of the wok and put aside. Now the vegetables and all the other ingredients are fried one after the other. The meat is put back in the wok at the end and all of the ingredients are mixed well and reheated quickly.

The taste can be further improved by marinating the meat before cooking. This involves putting the pieces of cut meat into typically Asian sauces flavored with some additional herbs and spices. Beef in particular becomes more tender and also tastier by marinating. Each type of meat harmonizes with specific spices, herbs and vegetables. The typically mild taste of chicken is complemented especially well by sweet flavors, while duck calls for much more savory seasoning. Pork is very versatile in its combination, blending well in simple and elegant as well as sophisticated recipes. Even lamb, with its own distinctive taste, can be complemented with both exotic flavors as well as with mild vegetables.

Fish and Seafood

Since the sea surrounds the Asian countries, Asian cooking has traditionally placed great importance on fish and seafood in. All seawater and freshwater fish, as well as mussels, prawns, lobsters, crayfish and particularly squids are ideal candidates for wok cooking. Fish is usually cut into bite-sized pieces before cooking, but can also be fried whole. If fish dishes are combined with vegetables, it is usual to start with cooking the vegetables, since most types of vegetables require a longer time to be cooked than fish. This avoids the fish getting overcooked. Fish and seafood generally go well with hot spices as well as sweet and sour flavors, vegetables or exotic fruit, such as for example pineapple or mango. There is a trick that makes any rather tough piece of squid tender: The tubes are cut open and placed with the inside facing the work surface. Diamond shapes are cut into the outside using a sharp knife. The carved pieces of squid open up during cooking, which also looks very decorative.

Many types of prawns, also referred to as shrimps, crevettes or gambas, are obtained from the world's seas and oceans. The tiger or giant prawns found in the subtropical waters of the Indian and Pacific Oceans are primarily used in Asian cooking. Prawns are removed from the shell by opening the underside. The upper edge of the prawn is cut open with a knife to remove the often-black length of intestine.

Marinating the pieces of fish before cooking will make them especially tasty. Typical Asian sauces such as fish, oyster, soy or hoisin sauce, but also rice wine can be used for marinating. The special character of each marinade is obtained with exotic herbs and spices such as lemon grass, chili and ginger or also honey, creating the special and characteristic charm of Asian cuisine.

Scallops have exquisitely tender meat. If possible, they should be bought in the shell, which has to be opened before use. The shell should be held with the flat side on top. A knife is then inserted between the upper and lower shell to sever the muscle holding them together. The 'beard' of gray fibers can then be removed and discarded, the red roe (the coral colored egg sac also referred to as corail) is detached and also used in cooking.

Mussels are subject to strict quality control and must be absolutely fresh. Make sure while shopping and preparing mussels that the shells are firmly closed or close again immediately when given a little knock. It is imperative that any open uncooked mussels are removed. During cooking however, the mussels should open; any mussels that remain closed during the cooking process must be discarded.

Notes on Ingredients

Alfalfa sprouts

From a forage plant also known as lucerne.
(Illustration 1)

Oyster sauce

A thick, brown sauce used for seasoning. It is quite salty and should be used sparingly. (Illustration 2)

Bamboo shoots

These are the young edible shoots of a certain bamboo variety. With their delicate, nutty flavor, they are very popular in Asian cooking, used as a warm or cold vegetable.

Bean curd

Also known as tofu, is a particularly nutritious plant-based food supplement obtained from cooked soybeans.

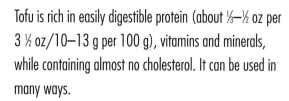

Tofu is rich in easily digestible protein (about ⅓–½ oz per 3 ½ oz/10–13 g per 100 g), vitamins and minerals, while containing almost no cholesterol. It can be used in many ways.

Since Asian cooking has become so popular in Europe, tofu has also become available in different flavors – from plain (natural taste) to savory, smoked or marinated.

Bonito flakes or powder

Made of dry saltwater fish, mainly tuna.

Chilli

Chilies are the pods of a variety of capsicum pepper plants. Depending on their color – green, yellow or red – these may vary from hot to mild. Another rule of thumb: the smaller, the hotter. The seeds are primarily responsible for the hotness. Removing the seeds beforehand will make the taste a little milder. (Illustration 3)

Curry

Curry is a mixture of spices that Asian housewives mix themselves according to taste and purpose. The guiding principle is to achieve a harmony between the five tastes – sweet, sour, bitter, mild, hot. If you feel like being really authentic, try roasting the dried spices such as cardamom, cumin, turmeric, pepper, cinnamon, cloves, chili and mace briefly in a pan without any oil (careful – they burn quickly), cool off and then grind using a mortar. This mixture can be kept for some time in closed glass containers stored away from light.

Curry pastes

These form the basis of many Thai dishes, containing their typical flavors. They are made of a great variety of spices and herbs and range from mild to hot depending on the composition. Grinding the ingredients using a mortar develops their full flavor.

Spring onions

Spring onions are milder than their regular larger and smaller relations. The name 'spring' refers to the fresh and tender green appearance rather than the time of harvest. The delicate little onions are available almost all year round.

Five-spice powder

The composition, based on fennel seed, clove, cardamom or pepper, star aniseed and cinnamon, varies according to country.

Galangal

Galangal is a member of the ginger family and, similar to ginger, this root is peeled before use and cut into thin slices or finely chopped. Although galangal is similar to ginger in its flavor, it is less hot.

Hoisin sauce

As far as well-known Asian sauces are concerned, this sauce comes immediately after soy sauce, particularly in Chinese cooking. Made on a soybean basis, it is produced in various flavors according to a traditional basic recipe.

Ginger

Ginger is an all-time favorite in Asia. Even the great Confucius always used ginger with his food, and he must have had a good reason for this. The yellow brown, oddly shaped roots are packed with antibacterial and digestive agents. If at all possible, ginger should be used fresh, to obtain the full flavor ranging from savory to hot.

Kaffir lime

The peel and leaves of the kaffir lime (also known as makrut) are used in Thai cooking to provide a lemon flavor. The peel is added to dishes finely chopped, while the leaves are either added whole and removed after cooking, or eaten with the food if they are added finely chopped. (Illustration 4)

Cardamom

The cardamom flavor calls to mind cinnamon and cloves. The seeds of this reed-like plant are used for seasoning. They are valued for their special flavor as well as their medicinal qualities. (Illustration 5)

Coconut milk

This is not the liquid contained in the coconut, but rather the liquid obtained from the coconut flesh. It is quite easy to make by finely grating the white inner lining of the nut and adding an equal quantity of boiling water. After leaving this to stand for a short period of time, the mixture can be pressed through a cloth. Dried coconut flakes (desiccated coconut) or unsweetened canned coconut milk can be used alternatively.

Coriander

Also known as 'Chinese parsley'. Only the appearance, but not the taste of these two herbs is similar. The whole plant is used in Asian cooking: the aromatic leaves, the peppercorn-sized seeds tasting of cinnamon and nutmeg (whole or ground) as well as the roots. This annual plant can be easily grown in any vegetable garden. (Illustration 6)

Cumin

Cumin is similar in appearance to the local European caraway seeds and also has a similar digestive effect. The taste is, however, very different, making it a little difficult to find a suitable substitute for this spice. If you want to know how cumin tastes, have a sip of bitters used for digestive purposes — this is where cumin is mainly used in Europe.

Turmeric

Also known as curcuma. This is what gives curry its typically yellow color, with a mild peppery, slightly bitter taste.

Mirin

Mirin is a slightly sweet rice wine. Dry sherry is a suitable substitute.

Miso

This is a seasoning paste made of rice, soybean sprouts or barley and soybeans, available in many varieties.

Mu-er mushrooms

Also known as cloud ear mushrooms due to their appearance, these are mostly dried and need to be soaked in water before use.

Nutmeg and mace

Nutmeg and mace are spices obtained from the same tree. The nut is the size of a walnut and is enclosed by the blossom or mace. Freshly ground nutmeg has a savory bitter aroma. Mace can be added to the food being cooked whole or roughly broken and removed before serving. (Illustration 1)

Nam prik

This is the Burmese equivalent of sambal. The paste mainly consists of chilies, garlic, shallots as well as shrimps or prawn paste.

Soy sauce

This absolutely essential sauce for Asian cooking is available in many flavors and two types — light and dark. The light sauce has a mild taste and is intended for flavoring food. The thicker dark sauce is more intensive and also makes food saltier.

Pimento

The seeds of the pimento tree taste like a cross between cloves and peppercorns and are called pimento. They should either be used whole or freshly crushed. Pimento is also known as allspice and is used together with bay leaves for the refinement fish and meat stocks. (Illustration 2)

Rau om

Also known as rice paddy herb or ngo om, with aromatic leaves that have a slightly sweet taste of cumin. Rau om is very popular in Thai and Vietnamese cuisine.

Saffron

Saffron is obtained from the stigmas of a crocus variety and is a very expensive spice.

Sambal oelek

This is a blisteringly hot chili paste that should be used sparingly. (Illustration 3)

Sesame oil

This very aromatic essence is obtained from raw seeds (light) for frying and from roasted seeds (dark) for seasoning.

Shiitake mushrooms

These are cultured mushrooms from Japan. They are aromatic and can be used almost completely. They are suitable for freezing and drying and most importantly, are not contaminated with pollutants.

Palm sugar

Palm sugar is used for seasoning sweet as well as savory dishes. It is available as pressed pieces and can be substituted by brown sugar if necessary.

Chopsticks

These are the normal eating utensils used in many Asian countries. In countries where the Chinese influence is less pronounced, such as Thailand, Indonesia, Malaysia or the Philippines, people mainly eat with a spoon, sometimes with a spoon and fork or simply with the fingers. Not all chopsticks are the same. But whatever the size or appearance, they all have the same aim: to make the person eating concentrate on the food, eat slowly, enjoy and digest well.

Star aniseed

Star aniseed looks like a star and tastes of anise. It can also be replaced by aniseed or fennel seeds.

Tamarind

This is a slightly sour date used for making sauces, pastes or purée. (Illustration 4)

Tempura flour

This particularly fine flour is used to make the typical deep-frying batter.

Thai basil

This has hardly anything in common with the basil we know in Europe. The leaves are firmer and the sharper taste is reminiscent of anise. (Illustration 5)

Garlic chives

Also known as Chinese chives, this is an integral part of Thai cooking. Smells like chives and tastes like garlic. (Illustration 6)

Tofu

See bean curd

Wonton pastry sheets

These are thin pastry sheets made of rice flour.

Water chestnuts

The dark brown, bulbous fruit of an aquatic plant. Outside Asia, water chestnuts are generally only available canned. They may be replaced by pieces of bamboo shoots.

Lemon grass

Lemon grass is a perennial fragrant grass, the stalks of which have a delicate lemon flavor that is diminished slightly on drying. In Europe, lemon grass is available in special shops either fresh, but usually dried whole, and recently also ground. If you cannot get hold of any lemon grass, use finely grated lemon peel.

Snow peas

These small light green pods containing sweet tasting peas are also known as mangetout. Although they are easy to grow in most vegetable gardens, they must be harvested in time. Their delicate taste is lost if they are picked too late and the pods can then no longer be eaten whole.

23

Soups

Soups are a delightful potpourri of delicacies in Asia. The nuances of even a very simple broth are harmonized according to a long tradition.

Sorrel Soup

1   Wash the sorrel, dry and chop coarsely. Cut the dates into small pieces. Drain the palm hearts and chop into small pieces. Heat the oil in a wok and briefly fry the sorrel with the dates and palm hearts.

2   Add the vegetable stock and season with salt, pepper, ginger and clove powder. Add the bean paste and allow the mixture to simmer for about 10 minutes. Add the coconut milk and allow to cook for another 1 to 2 minutes while stirring.

3   Roast the sesame seeds in a pan without any oil. Put the soup into small bowls and serve sprinkled with the sesame seeds.

Serves 4

14 oz/400 g sorrel

5 dried dates

3 ½ oz/100 g palm hearts, canned

3–4 tbsp peanut oil

2 cups/500 ml vegetable stock

salt

pepper

ginger and clove powder

2–3 tbsp hot black bean paste

1 cup/250 ml unsweetened coconut milk

2–3 tbsp sesame seeds

Preparation time: ca. 20 minutes
264 kcal/1110 kJ

Fish Soup with Tofu

1   Wash the fish filet, dry and cut into small cubes. Peel the cucumber, halve lengthways and remove the pips. Cut the cucumber into triangles.

2   Heat the oil in a wok and fry the fish cubes together with the cucumber pieces for 2 to 3 minutes. Add the onion-garlic and 8-herb mixture.

3   Add the stock and crumble the crab paste into the soup. Allow to dissolve while stirring. Season the soup with the soy sauce and aniseed liqueur. Allow the mixture to cook at a moderate temperature for about 10 minutes. Cut the tofu into small cubes and add about 3 minutes before the end of the cooking time. Serve the soup in small bowls.

Serves 4

1 ¼ lb/600 g fillet of plaice

1 cucumber

3–4 tbsp sesame oil

⅓ cup/ 3 ½ oz onion-garlic mixture (fresh or dried)

1 package 8-herb mixture (fresh or dried)

2 cups/450 ml fish stock (ready-to-use)

½ cube crab soup paste (ready-to-use)

2–3 tbsp soy sauce

4 tsp aniseed liqueur

7 oz/200 g tofu

Preparation time: ca. 35 minutes
306 kcal/1285 kJ

Asparagus Soup
with Shrimps

1 Bring the chicken broth to the boil. In the meantime, wash the asparagus and cut in half. Cook the asparagus in the boiling broth for about 5 minutes, remove and put aside.

2 Gut the shrimps. Wash and dry the shrimps. Peel and finely chop the shallots.

3 Heat the oil in a wok and slightly braise the shallots for 2 minutes. Add the asparagus, shrimps and broth. Allow the soup to cook for 3 minutes.

4 Remove the wok from the heat. Mix the cornstarch with a little water and add the smooth paste obtained to the soup and stir in well.

5 Reheat the soup and cook until it thickens slightly. Stir in the fish sauce, add salt and pepper.

6 Whisk the egg and add. Stir the egg into the soup vigorously until threads appear. Serve garnished with chives.

Serves 4

1 quart/1 l chicken broth

11 oz/300 g green asparagus tips

7 oz/200 g shrimps or prawns

4 shallots

1 tbsp oil

1 tbsp cornstarch

2 tbsp fish sauce

salt

pepper

1 egg

chives for garnishing

*Preparation time: ca. 20 minutes (plus cooking time)
100 kcal/418 kJ*

Serves 4

14 oz/400 g duck legs or leftover roast duck

1–2 tbsp peanut oil

3 red chilies

3 garlic cloves

3 shallots

3 tbsp fish sauce

3 ½ oz/100 g oyster mushrooms

2–3 tbsp chili sauce

2 cups/500 ml coconut milk

2 cups/500 ml duck stock (ready-to-use)

½ bunch Thai basil

Preparation time: ca. 25 minutes
553 kcal/2325 kJ

Hot Duck Soup

1 Remove the skin and bones from the duck legs and cut the meat into small pieces. Heat the oil in a wok and fry portions of the meat until brown. Take out and keep warm.

2 Halve the chilies, remove the seeds and wash under cold running water. Cut into strips. Peel the garlic and shallots and cut into slices.

3 Mix the chilies, garlic and shallots with the fish sauce and stir-fry in the oil left in the wok for 3 to 4 minutes.

4 Clean the oyster mushrooms, chop and add. Add the chili sauce, coconut milk and duck stock followed by the meat. Cook at a moderate temperature for about 6 to 7 minutes. Wash the basil, dry and cut into thin strips. Add to the soup and cook for about 2 minutes. Serve the soup in small bowls.

Serves 4

5 oz/150 g rice vermicelli

3 cups/750 ml lobster
stock (ready-to-use)

2–3 tbsp ginger juice

2–3 tbsp soy sauce

lemon-pepper seasoning

11 oz/300 g crayfish meat

2 eggs

*Preparation time: ca. 20 minutes
570 kcal/2396 kJ*

31

Rice Noodles with Crayfish

1 Place the noodles in sufficient warm water, until soft.
Transfer to a sieve, allow to drain well and rinse with cold
water.

2 Heat the lobster stock together with the ginger juice,
soy sauce and lemon-pepper seasoning in a wok. Cook the
noodles in this mixture for 3 to 5 minutes at a moderate
temperature.

3 Add the crayfish meat and warm up. Whisk the eggs
and slowly pour into the rice noodle mixture. Allow to set at
a moderate temperature for about 1 minute and then stir
gently. Serve the soup in small bowls.

Serves 4

1 onion

2 garlic cloves

1 red and 1 green chili

1 lemon grass stalk

1 piece fresh galangal
(ca. ⅓ in/1 cm)

2 tbsp red curry paste

1 tbsp peanut oil

3 kaffir lime leaves

2 cups/500 ml chicken
broth

1 ¼ cups/300 ml coconut
milk

1 cup/250 ml coconut
cream

fish sauce to taste

lime juice to taste

1 ¼ lb/600 g chicken
breast fillets

4 ½ oz/125 g field or
button mushrooms

2 tomatoes

3 spring onions

fresh coriander to taste

*Preparation time: ca. 20 minutes
(plus cooking time)
390 kcal/1638 kJ*

Hot Chicken Coconut Soup

1 Peel and finely chop the onions and garlic. Clean, wash and halve the chili, remove the base of the stalk and seeds and chop finely. Clean, wash and finely chop the lemon grass. Peel and finely chop the galangal.

2 Fry all of the vegetables with the curry paste in the peanut oil. Add the washed lime leaves as well as the chicken broth, simmer for 15 minutes. Stir in the coconut milk and cream and allow to simmer for 5 minutes. Add the fish sauce and lime juice to taste.

3 Cut the chicken breast into strips. Clean the mushrooms by brushing them and cut them into slices. Pour boiling water over the tomatoes, then remove the skin and the seeds, and cut into small cubes. Clean the spring onions, wash and cut into small pieces.

4 Add everything to the seasoning mixture and allow to cook for 5 minutes. Wash the coriander, shake dry and pluck the leaves from the stalks. Serve the chicken stew with a sprinkling of coriander leaves.

Serves 4

5 dried red chilies

2 small chopped onions

2 tbsp grated ginger

1 tbsp chopped lemon grass

8 kemiri nuts (candlenuts)

1 ½ tsp prawn paste

¼ tsp saffron powder

4 tbsp oil

1 ¼ lb/600 g raw prawns

2 cups/500 ml coconut milk

3 ½ oz/100 g soybean sprouts

generous 1 lb/500 g thin fresh rice noodles

10 Korean mint leaves

Preparation time: ca. 25 minutes (plus soaking time, plus cooking time)
488 kcal/2048 kJ

34

Prawns with Ginger

1 Soak the red chilies in hot water for 15 minutes. Drain, and purée with onion, ginger, lemon grass, nuts, prawn paste, saffron and 2 tablespoons of oil.

2 Gut and wash the prawns. Fry the heads and shells in 1 tablespoon of oil until they turn dark orange. Add 3 cups/750 ml water and allow to simmer for 30 minutes without a lid. Remove, and then strain the broth.

3 Fry the seasoning paste in 1 tablespoon of oil in the wok for 6 minutes. Allow to simmer with prawn broth and coconut milk for 5 minutes. Add prawns and cook until orange. Heat the drained soybean sprouts in the mixture.

4 Keep the noodles in boiling water for 30 seconds, drain and add. Serve the soup garnished with prawns and washed mint.

Coconut Soup with Duck

1   Wash the meat, dry and cut into strips. Peel and finely chop the garlic cloves. Peel the shallots and cut into cubes. Clean the oyster mushrooms, wash and cut into pieces.

2   Wash the beans, dry and cut into small pieces. Peel the ginger and grate. Peel the coriander roots and cut into slices. Peel the kaffir lime and chop the peel finely. Then filet the lime. Wash the chili, halve lengthways, remove the seeds and cut into strips.

3   Heat the oil in a wok and fry the meat with the garlic and the shallots. Add the mushrooms and beans after about 4 minutes. Add the ginger, coriander root, kaffir limes, lime filets and chili and then fry for a short time.

4   Add Asian-style stock, coconut milk and about 1 ¼ cups/300 ml water and allow to cook gently at a moderate temperature for about 6 minutes. Add curry paste to taste. Wash the Thai basil, dry and remove the leaves. Serve the soup in small bowls, garnished with basil.

Serves 4

1 ¼ lb/600 g duck breast filets without skin

3 garlic cloves

2 shallots

3 ½ oz/100 g oyster mushrooms

3 ½ oz/100 g yard-long beans

1 piece fresh ginger (1 ¼ in/3 cm)

1 piece fresh coriander root (1 ¼ in/3 cm)

2 kaffir limes

1 lime

1 red chili

3 tbsp peanut oil

1 ⅔ cups/400 ml Asian-style stock

2 cups/500 ml coconut milk

1 tbsp green curry paste (ready-to-use)

Thai basil for garnishing

Preparation time: ca. 50 minutes
657 kcal/2762 kJ

35

Wonton Soup

1   Drain the mushrooms. Squeeze the mushrooms a little to remove some more liquid. Peel, gut and finely chop the prawns.

2   Mix the prawns, mushrooms, ground meat, salt, soy sauce, sesame oil, half of the spring onions, ginger and water chestnuts thoroughly.

3   Use the wonton pastry sheets quickly, covering unused sheets with a damp cloth to keep them from becoming dry.

4   Put 1 heaped teaspoon of the filling in the middle of a piece of dough. Moisten the edges of the wrapper with some water; fold the square into a triangle, pressing the edges together a little. Place the little, wrapped parcels on a flour-dusted wooden board.

5   Bring plenty of water to the boil. Allow the dumplings to cook for 4 to 5 minutes in the vigorously boiling water. Boil the chicken broth in a separate pot. Add the remaining finely chopped spring onions.

6   Remove the boiled wonton from the water using a skimming ladle, allow to drain and keep warm. Put the wonton in bowls or deep plates and pour the boiling broth over them. Serve the soup straight away.

Serves 4

3 soaked dried Chinese mushrooms

7 oz/200 g raw prawns

7 oz/200 g ground pork

1 pinch of salt

1 tbsp soy sauce

1 tsp sesame oil

5 finely chopped spring onions

1 piece ginger, freshly grated

2 tbsp chopped water chestnuts

7 oz/200 g wonton wrappers (ready-to-use)

1 quart/1 l chicken broth

Preparation time: ca. 40 minutes (plus cooking time)
243 kcal/1023 kJ

Vegetables

Freshness and simplicity are essential to Asian cooking, this is why great importance is attached to vegetables and aromatic herbs. In a wok, these ingredients can be cooked within minutes, without the loss of taste, vitamins or nutrients.

Pak Choi with Egg

1   Clean the pak choi (sometimes spelled bok choy), wash and allow to drain well. Cut the vegetables into bite-sized pieces. Peel the onions and cut into small cubes. Halve the chilies, remove the inner partitions and seeds, wash them under running water and finely dice them.

2   Heat the oil in a wok and gently braise the diced onions and chilies while stirring. Add the pak choi and braise for a short time. Pour in the coconut milk, the soy sauce and the tomato cubes. Allow to stew for about 10 to 15 minutes. Season with salt and pepper.

3   Drain the eggs well and halve them. Arrange the vegetables on a dish and serve garnished with the eggs.

Serves 4

1 ¼–1 ½ lb/600–700 g pak choi

2 onions

4 chilies

3–4 tbsp peanut oil

1 ⅓ cups/300 g diced tomatoes, canned

4–5 tbsp soy sauce

2–3 tbsp coconut milk

salt

pepper, freshly ground

4–5 quail's eggs, boiled, in a jar

Preparation time: ca. 30 minutes
235 kcal/990 kJ

Mixed Fried Vegetables

1   Peel the onions and garlic cloves and cut into small cubes. Clean the eggplants and zucchini, wash, halve lengthways and cut into finger-thick triangles. Skin the tomatoes, halve, remove the seeds and cut into small pieces. Cut the sweet peppers in half, remove the seeds, wash and cut coarsely.

2   Heat the oil in a wok and stir-fry the vegetables separately for about 2 to 3 minutes. Put all of the vegetables in the wok and season with salt, pepper, mustard seeds and cumin.

3   Clean, wash and finely chop the herbs. Add to the vegetables and then pour in the vegetable stock. Allow to simmer for about 2 to 3 minutes. Roast the sesame seeds in a pan without any oil and sprinkle over the vegetables.

Serves 4

3 red onions

2 garlic cloves

2 small eggplants

2 small zucchini

4 beef tomatoes

2 sweet peppers

4 tbsp sesame oil, salt

pepper, freshly ground

mustard seeds

cumin powder

1–2 stalks Thai basil

1–2 stalks lemon grass or 1 tbsp dried lemon grass

2 cups/500 ml vegetable stock

2–3 tbsp hulled sesame seeds

Preparation time: ca. 25 minutes
480 kcal/2017 kJ

Steamed Zucchini Pyramids with Shrimp Paste

Serves 4

3 thick zucchini

1 bunch coriander

1 tbsp finely grated ginger

4 tbsp shrimp paste

Preparation time: ca. 30 minutes
41 kcal/172 kJ

1 Wash the zucchini, dry, clean and cut into very thin slices. Wash the coriander and shake dry thoroughly, pluck the leaves and cut some of them finely. Mix the ginger with shrimp paste and 2 tablespoons of water.

2 Line the bamboo baskets with coriander leaves. Spread some of the paste on the zucchini slices and arrange on top of each other as pyramids (about 2 in/ 5 cm high).

3 Put the zucchini pyramids into the bamboo baskets and sprinkle with coriander leaves.

4 Heat some water in a wok, place the bamboo baskets over it and steam for about 15 minutes with the lid on.

Steamed Tomatoes Stuffed with Cabbage and Ginger

1 Wash the tomatoes, dry, cut off the lid and scoop out the insides. Remove the outer cabbage leaves, halve the cabbage, cut out the stalk part and chop the leaves into thin strips. Peel the ginger and cut into fine slices.

2 Heat the oil in a wok and braise the cabbage strips with the ginger powder, hoisin sauce and fish sauce until soft. Stuff the tomatoes with the cabbage strips. Put three tomatoes in each bamboo basket and sprinkle with sliced ginger.

3 Heat some water in a wok and place the baskets on top of each other in the wok. Cover the wok with a lid. Exchange the uppermost basket with the bottom basket after 10 minutes and allow to steam for a further 10 minutes.

4 Finally drizzle some coriander oil over the tomatoes and sprinkle with the finely chopped coriander leaves.

Serves 4

12 medium size tomatoes
½ small white cabbage
3 ½ oz/100 g ginger root
1 tbsp vegetable oil
2 tbsp ginger powder
1 tbsp hoisin sauce
2 tbsp fish sauce
coriander oil to taste
½ bunch coriander

Preparation time: ca. 40 minutes
122 kcal/512 kJ

43

Bamboo Shoots with Peppers and Alfalfa

Serves 4

generous 1 lb/500 g bamboo shoots

2 red and 2 green peppers

1 sprig coriander

4 tbsp vegetable oil

1 tbsp shrimp paste

2 tbsp hoisin sauce

3 ½ oz/100 g alfalfa sprouts

Preparation time: ca. 25 minutes
146 kcal/611 kJ

1 Slice the bamboo shoots diagonally, wash, clean and de-seed the peppers and cut them into strips. Wash the coriander, shake dry, pluck the leaves and chop finely.

2 Heat the oil in a wok, fry the peppers briefly and then add the bamboo shoots. Add the shrimp paste and the hoisin sauce, mix well and continue frying.

3 Finally, gently mix in the alfalfa sprouts, toss and serve sprinkled with coriander leaves.

44

Fried Shiitake Mushrooms with Spring Onions in Sesame Oil

Serves 4

1 ¼ lb/600 g fresh shiitake mushrooms

1 bunch spring onions

4 tbsp roasted sesame oil

1 tbsp sesame seeds

2 tbsp oyster sauce

4 tbsp rice wine

Preparation time: ca. 15 minutes
183 kcal/767 kJ

1 Do not wash the shiitake mushrooms, but wipe them with a piece of paper towel. Only remove the bottom ends of the stems. Wash the spring onions, dry, clean and cut into rings.

2 Heat the sesame oil in a wok and fry the mushrooms at a high temperature until they are done. Then add the spring onion rings and also fry a little. Sprinkle with sesame seeds and roast gently.

3 Finally add the oyster sauce and pour in the rice wine. Cook briefly, until the liquid has just evaporated.

Spinach with Roasted Garlic and Soybean Sprouts

1 Clean the spinach, wash thoroughly under running water and gently shake dry. Peel the garlic cloves and cut into thin strips.

2 Heat the oil in a wok and fry the garlic until golden brown, add the soybean sprouts and toss the mixture gently. Add the spinach and allow to collapse. Season with fish sauce.

Serves 4

2 ¼ lb/1 kg fresh leaf spinach

5 garlic cloves

3 tbsp peanut oil

generous 1 lb/500 g soybean sprouts

2 tbsp fish sauce

Preparation time: ca. 15 minutes
180 kcal/754 kJ

Deep-fried Zucchini

Serves 4

1 ¾ lb/800 g zucchini

generous 1 cup/125 g
ground cashews

7 tbsp grated Parmesan
cheese

½ bunch coriander

1 egg

1 pinch of salt, pepper

¼ cup/60 ml peanut oil

1 ⅔ cup/400 ml sour cream

6 tbsp yogurt

1 garlic clove

1 small red pepper

ginger and clove powder

Preparation time: ca. 30 minutes
816 kcal/3430 kJ

1 Wash the zucchini, dry and cut into thin slices lengthwise. Mix the cashews with the cheese. Wash, dry and finely chop the coriander leaves, and fold into the cheese mixture.

2 Whisk the egg in a bowl, add salt and pepper. Dip the zucchini slices in the egg mixture and then turn them over in the cheese mixture. Press the coating on a little.

3 Heat the oil in a wok and fry the zucchini slices until golden brown.

4 Mix the sour cream with the yogurt in a bowl. Peel the garlic clove, press and add. Wash the pepper, halve, de-seed, dice very finely and mix with the dip. Season to taste with salt, pepper, ginger and cumin powder. Serve the zucchini slices with the dip.

Deep-fried Endive

1 Clean the endive leaves, wash under running water and drain well. Dry the endive leaves and cut into pieces about 2 in/5 cm long.

2 Beat the eggs white until stiff. Whisk the yolk and lift under the beaten egg white. Fold in salt, flour and cornstarch. Immerse the endive leaves in the egg batter and deep-fry in peanut oil until golden brown.

3 For the first sauce, heat the orange juice, remove from the heat and stir in peanut oil, paprika powder, chili powder and coriander leaves.

4 For the second sauce, heat the soy sauce a little and add the spice powder with the sugar. Continue to heat while stirring until the sugar has dissolved.

5 For the third sauce, mix the vinegar with sesame oil, sugar and some salt. Clean, wash and finely chop the spring onions and stir into the sauce.

6 Serve the three sauces together with the well-drained endive.

Serves 4

generous 1 lb/500 g endive
8 egg whites
2 egg yolks
1 pinch of salt
2 tbsp flour
1 tbsp cornstarch
peanut oil for deep-frying
7 tbsp/100 ml orange juice
1 tbsp peanut oil
1 tbsp each paprika, chili powder
1 tbsp chili powder
¾ oz/20 g coriander leaves
7 tbsp/100 ml light soy sauce
1 tbsp five-spice powder
2–3 tbsp cane sugar
7 tbsp/100 ml raspberry vinegar
1 tbsp each of sesame oil and sugar
¼ bunch spring onions

Preparation time: ca. 30 minutes
367 kcal/1541 kJ

47

48

Spring Rolls

1   For the dough, separate the egg white from the yolk of one egg, put the yolk aside. Whisk the egg white with the other eggs and about 1 ½ cups/350 ml of water. Add salt, oil and flour and mix until the dough is smooth. Allow the dough to rest for 30 minutes.

2   Allow some butter to froth up in a wok and then bake very thin light crêpes, one after the other. Remove and put aside.

3   For the stuffing, peel and finely chop the onion and the garlic. Drain the bamboo shoots and cut into narrow strips. Peel the carrots and also cut into narrow strips. Wash the sprouts.

4   Heat up some butter in the wok. Braise the garlic and onion a little. Add the carrots and fry for 3 minutes. Add the sprouts and fry for another 2 minutes.

5   Fill the crêpe wrappers with the vegetable mixture. Roll up firmly and brush with egg yolk. Fry the rolls in a little butter until they are golden brown all over.

Serves 4

4 eggs

1 pinch of salt

2 tbsp oil

generous 1 ⅓ cups/200 g flour

butter for frying

1 large onion

3 garlic cloves

1 can of bamboo shoots (ca. 7 oz/200 g)

2 carrots

3 ½ oz/100 g bean sprouts

Preparation time: ca. 30 minutes (plus standing time)
303 kcal/1271 kJ

49

Sweet and Sour Peppers

Serves 4

2 each red, yellow, and green peppers

4 tomatoes

6 garlic cloves

½ bunch parsley

3 tbsp peanut oil

4 tbsp rice wine

4 tbsp soy sauce

1 tbsp sugar

aniseed, coriander, and ginger powder

Preparation time: ca. 20 minutes
255 kcal/1072 kJ

1   Wash, clean, de-seed the peppers and cut into thin strips. Slash the skin of the tomatoes crosswise, immerse in boiling water for a short time, rinse with cold water, peel and cut into wedges.

2   Peel the garlic cloves and squeeze using a press. Wash, dry and finely chop the parsley. Heat the oil in a wok and gently braise the vegetables. Add the rice wine and the soy sauce.

3   Allow to simmer briefly and season to taste with sugar, aniseed, coriander and ginger powder. Arrange on plates and serve.

50

Serves 4

4 ½ oz/125 g broccoli

4 ½ oz/125 g cauliflower

½ cucumber

3 carrots

4 ½ oz/125 g Chinese cabbage

4 ½ oz/125 g pak choi

½ cup/100 g corn, canned

2 cups/500 ml rice vinegar

2 tbsp sugar

salt

5 garlic cloves

2 onions

6 red dried chilies

⅓ cup/75 ml peanut oil

2 tbsp sesame seeds

Preparation time: ca. 35 minutes
319 kcal/1340 kJ

51

Thai Vegetables

1 Clean the vegetables, wash, dry and chop into small pieces. Drain the corn well using a strainer. Bring to the boil the vinegar, sugar and some salt in 2 cups/500 ml of water. Blanch portions of the vegetables in this liquid.

2 Peel and roughly chop the onions and garlic cloves. Finely grind in a mortar together with the chilies. Heat the oil in a wok and fry the paste for about 3 minutes.

3 Add the vegetables as well as the liquid they were cooked in and allow to simmer at a moderate temperature for about 2 minutes. Roast the sesame seeds in a pan without any oil.

4 Serve the vegetables on plates, sprinkled with the sesame seeds.

Serves 4

4 small eggplants

7 tbsp oil

3–4 garlic cloves

1 onion

6 tsp brown sugar

6 tsp soy sauce

6 tsp cider vinegar

1 tbsp dry sherry

*Preparation time: ca. 10 minutes
(plus frying time)
77 kcal/323 kJ*

Sweet Garlic Eggplants

1 Clean and wash the eggplants. Remove the base of the stalk, and then halve lengthwise. Cut the eggplant halves into cubes of about 1 x 1 in/3 x 3 cm.

2 Heat 3 tablespoons of the oil in a wok, tilting the wok carefully to distribute the oil around the edges. Put half of the eggplant cubes in the wok, stir-fry for 5 minutes at a high temperature, until the vegetables are brown and the oil has been absorbed completely.

3 Allow the eggplants to drain on a paper towel. Stir-fry the other half of the eggplant cubes in 3 tablespoons of oil, remove and allow to drain.

4 Heat up the rest of the oil in the wok. Peel and finely chop the garlic and onion, and fry in hot oil for 3 minutes. Sprinkle with the sugar and allow to caramelize a little. Add soy sauce, vinegar and sherry, and bring to the boil while stirring.

5 Put the eggplant cubes back in the wok and allow to simmer for 3 minutes until the sauce is almost completely absorbed. Serve the eggplants with white rice.

Serves 4

3 ½ oz/100 g Chinese cabbage

4 ½ oz/125 g carrots

4 ½ oz/125 g fresh shiitake mushrooms

4 ½ oz/125 g snow peas

1 ¾ oz/50 g ginger

2 garlic cloves

2 red chilies

3 ½ oz/100 g canned bamboo shoots

5 oz/150 g pineapple

4 tbsp sunflower oil

4 tbsp rice vinegar

4 tbsp light soy sauce

4 tbsp sherry

2 tbsp sugar

generous ¾ cup/200 ml chicken broth

1 tsp cornstarch

Preparation time: ca. 30 minutes
399 kcal/1676 kJ

54

Sweet and Sour Vegetables

1 Wash the Chinese cabbage, dry and halve the leaves lengthways. Then cut into ¾ in/2 cm wide strips. Peel the carrots and cut into thin slices. Wipe the mushrooms with a piece of paper towel and cut them in half. Wash the snow peas and also cut in half.

2 Peel the ginger and cut into very thin slices. Peel and finely chop the garlic cloves. Wash and de-seed the chilies and cut into strips.

3 Drain the bamboo shoots in a strainer. Peel the pineapple, remove the stalk and cut the flesh into small pieces.

4 Heat the oil in a wok and fry the carrots with the mushrooms, snow peas and Chinese cabbage. Add the ginger, garlic and chili and fry again briefly. Add the bamboo shoots, pineapple, vinegar, soy sauce, sherry and sugar. Add ¾ of the broth and mix.

5 Mix the cornstarch with the remaining cold broth, pour over the vegetables and stir in straight away. Allow to simmer for 4 minutes. Serve in small bowls.

Scrambled Eggs with Mushrooms

1 Completely cover the mushrooms with hot water. Allow to stand for about 15 minutes.

2 Wash and de-seed the chili, and then cut into thin strips. Peel and finely chop the ginger. Clean and wash the spring onions, and then cut into rings. Wash and dry the coriander and pluck off the leaves.

3 Drain the mushrooms in a strainer and cut into pieces. Whisk the eggs and mix in the soy sauce, pepper and peanut oil.

4 Heat the wok and add sunflower oil. Fry the mushrooms for a short time. Add the remaining ingredients, except for the eggs and the coriander, and mix with the mushrooms. Pour in the egg mixture and cook until it starts to set. Move the set egg mixture towards the edge of the wok.

5 Serve the scrambled eggs sprinkled with coriander leaves.

Serves 4

3 dried morels
3 dried shiitake mushrooms
1 red chili
⅓ oz/10 g ginger
2 spring onions
2 sprigs coriander
4 eggs
2 tsp soy sauce
1 pinch of pepper
1 tsp peanut oil
2 tbsp sunflower oil

Preparation time: ca. 30 minutes
230 kcal/966 kJ

Soybean Sprouts with Oranges

Serves 4

9 oz/250 g soybean sprouts

9 oz/250 g mixed pickles in a jar

3–4 tbsp sesame oil

2–3 oranges

9 oz/250 g smoked tofu

salt

pepper, freshly ground

4 tbsp soy sauce

1 tub of fresh cress

Preparation time: ca. 20 minutes
248 kcal/1042 kJ

1 Rinse the soybean sprouts under cold running water. Transfer to a sieve and allow to drain well. Drain the mixed pickles thoroughly.

2 Heat the oil in a wok and stir-fry the vegetables for a short time. Peel and fillet the oranges, removing the white skin. Cut out the orange fillets with a sharp knife and chop into small pieces.

3 Cut the tofu into cubes. Add the tofu and the orange pieces to the vegetables and season with salt, pepper and soy sauce. Allow to simmer for about 2 minutes.

4 Wash and dry the cress, and then cut some off. Serve in small bowls garnished with cress.

Szechuan Cucumbers with Bulgur

1 Wash the cucumbers, halve, remove the pips and slice diagonally. Clean the spring onions and cut into fine rings.

2 Peel and finely chop the ginger and the garlic cloves. Wash, de-seed and finely dice the chili.

3 Heat the oil and stir-fry the vegetables for about 6 to 7 minutes. Add the sugar, soy sauce and the Szechuan seasoning. Also add the chili oil.

4 Allow to simmer for 6 to 8 minutes. In the meantime, prepare the bulgur according to the instructions on the package. Carefully combine the bulgur with the other ingredients in the wok and serve in small bowls.

Serves 4

2 medium size cucumbers

1 bunch spring onions

1 piece of fresh ginger (1 ½ in/4 cm)

2 garlic cloves

1 red chili

3–4 tbsp sesame oil

1 tbsp cane sugar

2–3 tbsp soy sauce

1–2 tsp Szechuan seasoning (ready-to-use)

1 tbsp chili oil

generous 1 cup/150 g bulgur wheat

Preparation time: ca. 25 minutes
313 kcal/1315 kJ

Rice & Noodles

No dish is served without rice or noodles in Asia. Whether you are preparing a simple everyday meal or a sumptuous feast: in combination with typical Far Eastern flavors and the finest ingredients, rice and noodle dishes are more than just a simple side dish. See for yourself!

Serves 4

½–¾ cup/100–150 g rice

3 cups/750 ml veal stock
(ready-to-use)

1 cup/250 ml Asian-style
stock (ready-to-use)

2–3 tbsp soy sauce

2–3 tbsp rice wine

9 oz/250 g pork fillet

1 bunch spring onions

2–3 tbsp sesame oil

7 oz/200 g green
asparagus in a jar

salt

pepper

ginger and garlic powder

½ tub of fresh cress

Preparation time: ca. 35 minutes
370 kcal/1555 kJ

Rice with Pork Filet

1   Put the rice in a sieve and pour hot water over it. Mix the veal stock with the Asian-style stock, the soy sauce and the rice wine. Put the mixture in a pot, add the rice and bring to the boil. Allow to cook at a moderate temperature for about 15 to 20 minutes.

2   Wash the pork fillet, dry and cut into thin slices. Clean and wash the spring onions and cut into rings.

3   Heat the oil in a wok and stir-fry the spring onions with the pork fillet for about 4 to 5 minutes. Put the asparagus in a strainer and allow to drain well. Cut into bite-sized pieces and add to the meat. Heat and season to taste with the spices.

4   Gently mix the meat and the asparagus with the rice, and serve in small bowls sprinkled with cress.

Rice with Chicken Breast

1   Roast the rice in a pan without oil. Allow to cool off and grind coarsely in a mill suitable for grinding grain.

2   Heat the stock with the rice wine and soy sauce. Clean, wash and chop the lemon grass and stir in with the five-spice powder. Peel and dice the turnips. Clean, wash and chop the beans into small pieces. Add the vegetables to the boiling stock and allow to simmer for 7 minutes. Remove and allow to drain.

3   Heat the oil in a wok and fry the meat. Cut the bitter melon in cubes and add to the meat together with the vegetables and the pine kernels. Fry for 3 minutes. Stir in the rice and season to taste with duck sauce.

Serves 4

1 ¼ cups/250 g short grain rice

1 ¼ cups/300 ml Asian-style stock

5 tbsp rice wine

5 tbsp soy sauce

2 stalks lemon grass

2 tbsp five-spice powder

4 small turnips

7 oz/200 g yard-long beans

2 chicken breast fillets in slices

5 tbsp sesame oil

7 oz/200 g bitter melon

3 tbsp pine kernels

4 tbsp duck sauce (ready-to-use)

Preparation time: ca. 50 minutes
632 kcal/2656 kJ

Fried Rice with Chicken

1   Peel and finely chop the garlic cloves. Clean the spring onions, wash and cut into rings. Wash the cucumber and cut into strips. Skin the tomatoes and dice.

2   Heat the oil in a wok and fry the meat gently until it is done. Remove and keep warm.

3   Whisk the eggs and stir-fry in the oil left in the wok from frying. Add the rice with the garlic and the meat and heat up while stirring.

4   Stir in the fish sauce, pepper and sugar. Put the rice in a bowl and serve garnished with spring onions, cucumber strips and tomato cubes.

Serves 4

2–3 garlic cloves

8 spring onions

½ cucumber

5 tomatoes

3 tbsp oil

7 oz/200 g sliced chicken breast

3 eggs

2 cups/400 g steamed jasmine rice

3 tbsp fish sauce

white pepper

1 tbsp sugar

Preparation time: ca. 15 minutes
(plus frying time)
568 kcal/2384 kJ

Korean Noodles with Vegetables

1   Pour boiling water over the black mushrooms and allow to soak for 10 minutes. Then drain the mushrooms.

2   Cook the noodles in water according to the directions on the package. Drain and rinse thoroughly under cold running water, until the noodles are cold. This removes any excess starch. Shorten the noodles as required.

3   Peel and finely chop the garlic and the ginger. Clean, wash and chop the spring onions, cut 2 spring onions into 2 in/5 cm long pieces. Peel the carrots and cut into long, thin strips.

4   Heat 1 tablespoon of sesame oil with the vegetable oil in a wok. Stir-fry the garlic, ginger and the chopped spring onions for 3 minutes at medium heat. Clean, wash and drain the pak choi and then cut into small pieces.

5   Add the carrot strips and fry for 1 minute. Add the drained noodles, remaining spring onions, pak choi, remaining sesame oil, soy sauce, mirin and sugar. Mix and allow to simmer for 2 minutes covered with a lid. Add the mushrooms and continue to cook for another 2 minutes with the lid on. Sprinkle with sesame and seaweed and serve immediately.

Serves 4

4 tbsp dried black mushrooms

11 oz/300 g Korean noodles

3 garlic cloves

1 piece of fresh ginger (ca. 2 in/5 cm)

6 spring onions

3 carrots

3 tbsp sesame oil

2 tbsp vegetable oil

generous 1 lb/500 g pak choi or 9 oz/250 g spinach

¼ cup/60 ml Japanese soy sauce

2 tbsp mirin

1 tsp sugar

2 tbsp sesame seeds and seaweed powder

Preparation time: ca. 30 minutes (plus frying time)
260 kcal/1092 kJ

63

Steamed Rice Balls with Shrimp Stuffing

Serves 4

1 cup/200 g basmati rice

7 oz/200 g shrimps without shell

8 tbsp fish sauce (ready-to-use)

½ tsp finely grated ginger

1 tsp chili flakes

juice of 1 lime

3 finely chopped red chilies

1 tbsp chopped coriander

Preparation time: ca. 35 minutes
174 kcal/729 kJ

1 Cook the basmati rice according to the instructions on the package and leave to cool. For the stuffing, mix the shrimps with the fish sauce and the finely grated ginger. Form the rice balls with moist hands, make a dent in the middle, put the stuffing inside and close again. Make 12 balls in this manner.

2 Put the balls in a bamboo basket and sprinkle with chili flakes. Bring some water to the boil in a wok and stack the baskets on top of each other in the wok. Cover the wok with a lid.

3 Exchange the uppermost and the bottom basket after 15 minutes. Steam for a total of 30 minutes. For the dip, mix the fish sauce with lime juice, chilies and coriander.

64

Fried Rice with Peppers and Shiitake Mushrooms

Serves 4

1 ¼ cups/250 g long grain rice

7 oz/200 g dried shiitake mushrooms

2 red peppers

1 bunch spring onions

4 tbsp vegetable oil

2 tbsp light soy sauce

2 tbsp fish sauce

Preparation time: ca. 25 minutes
365 kcal/1527 kJ

1 Cook the rice according to the directions on the package and put aside. Soak the shiitake mushrooms in water. Cut the peppers into bite-sized pieces. Halve the spring onions lengthwise and cut into pieces.

2 Heat the oil in a wok and first fry the spring onions. Then add the pieces of chopped pepper and continue to fry for a short time. Cut the drained shiitake mushrooms in smaller pieces if necessary, add to the vegetables, and also fry. Season with soy sauce and with fish sauce. Finally add the cooked rice and continue to fry until the rice is heated through properly.

Ginger Rice Balls

1 Cook the basmati rice according to the instructions on the package and leave to cool off. Peel and slice the ginger, chop the coriander. Peel and finely chop 3 shallots, fry in hot oil until crispy, and remove. Mix with the candied ginger and some coriander leaves to make the stuffing.

2 Line the bamboo baskets with coriander and ginger. Form small rice balls with moist hands, make a dent in the middle, add some of the stuffing and shape into a ball again.

3 Put the rice balls in the bamboo baskets, slice the remaining shallot and sprinkle over the balls. Heat water in a wok, put the bamboo baskets on top and steam for 10 minutes with the lid on.

4 Pour a little sweet and sour sauce over the balls and serve the rest of the sauce as a dip.

Serves 4

1 cup/200 g basmati rice

3 ½ oz/100 g ginger root

1 bunch coriander

4 shallots

2 tbsp vegetable oil

2 tbsp chopped candied ginger

6 tbsp sweet & sour sauce (ready-to-use)

Preparation time: ca. 40 minutes
207 kcal/866 kJ

65

Serves 4

1 ⅔ cups/400 ml Asian-style stock

11 oz/300 g thin rice noodles

generous 1 lb/500 g tofu

3 red chilies

3 tbsp sesame oil

2 stalks lemon grass

1 piece of fresh ginger (⅓ in/1 cm)

8 shallots

3 kaffir lime leaves

3 tbsp tomato juice

3 tbsp fish sauce (ready-to-use)

2 tbsp palm sugar

2 tbsp lemon juice

garlic chives for garnishing

Preparation time: ca. 35 minutes
338 kcal/1421 kJ

Fried Rice Noodles

1 Heat the stock, put the rice noodles in it and allow the noodles to soak up some liquid for about 10 minutes. Cut the tofu into cubes. Wash the chilis, halve lengthwise, remove the seeds and cut into rings. Heat the oil and braise the tofu with the chilies.

2 Add the washed and dried lemon grass. Peel the ginger and grate. Peel the shallots, dice and add to the tofu together with the ginger. Wash, dry and finely chop the lime leaves. Add the leaves, tomato juice, fish sauce, palm sugar and lemon juice.

3 Wash and dry the garlic chives. Mix the rice noodles with the tofu and serve in small bowls garnished with garlic chives.

Thread Noodles with Mushrooms

1 Put the noodles (also known as cellophane noodles) in warm water until they are soft. Drain well and cut into lengths of 1 ¼ to 1 ½ in/3 to 4 cm.

2 Halve the peppers and the chilies, de-seed and wash. Cut into small cubes. Clean the mushrooms and cut into pieces. Peel and finely chop the garlic cloves and the ginger.

3 Heat the oil in a wok and stir-fry the vegetables for about 3 to 4 minutes in batches. Add the noodles and stir-fry for about 1 minute.

4 Season to taste with the spices and the chili sauce. Add the mushroom stock. Cook at a moderate temperature for about 4 to 5 minutes. Arrange the noodles with the mushrooms and vegetables and serve.

Serves 4

3 ½ oz/100 g bean thread noodles

1 red and 1 yellow pepper

3–4 hot chilies

11 oz/300 g oyster mushrooms

3 garlic cloves

1 piece of fresh ginger (¾ in/2 cm)

6–7 tbsp sesame oil

salt

pepper

mustard powder

1 tbsp chili sauce

½ cup/125 ml mushroom stock (ready-to-use)

Preparation time: ca. 25 minutes
289 kcal/1215 kJ

67

Four-Colored Rice

1   Cook the rice in sufficient boiling salted water according to the instructions on the package. Pour off the liquid and allow to drain well.

2   For the green rice, heat the sesame oil in a wok and fry the roughly chopped spinach and the peas briefly. Add the vegetable stock and the soy sauce, and cook for about 3 to 5 minutes at a moderate temperature. Season to taste with salt, pepper, onion and garlic powder and nutmeg. Carefully add one quarter of the cooked rice. Take out and keep warm.

3   For the purple rice, put the beets in a strainer and allow to drain well, keeping the drained liquid. Dice the beets. Put in the wok together with the liquid and heat. Season to taste with cardamom and clove powder and fold in another quarter portion of the rice. Take out and keep warm.

4   For the orange-colored rice, place the pumpkin in a strainer and allow to drain well. Then cut into small cubes. Peel the bananas and cut into small cubes. Drain and finely chop the apricots. Heat the sesame oil and stir-fry the pumpkin and banana cubes together with the apricots for 1 to 2 minutes. Season to taste with curry paste and carefully fold in another quarter of the rice. Remove and keep warm.

5   For the red rice, mix the diced tomatoes with the paprika paste, salt, pepper and sugar. Heat the sesame oil in the wok and warm up the tomato mixture for 1 to 2 minutes while stirring. Fold in the rest of the rice and heat up. Serve as four rice balls on plates.

Serves 4

2 ½ cups/500 g rice
salt

For the green rice:

2–3 tbsp sesame oil
3 ½ oz/100 g leaf spinach (frozen)
⅔ cup/100 g peas (frozen)
½ cup/125 ml vegetable stock
2–3 tbsp soy sauce
pepper
onion and garlic powder
nutmeg

For the purple rice:

11 oz/300 g beets in a jar
cardamom and clove powder

For the orange-colored rice:

7 oz/200 g sweet & sour pickled pumpkin
2 bananas
2–3 apricots, canned
2–3 tbsp sesame oil
1–2 tbsp yellow curry paste

For the red rice:

11 oz/300 g puréed tomatoes with onions and garlic (ready-to-use)
4–5 tbsp paprika paste
pepper
sugar
2–3 tbsp sesame oil

*Preparation time: ca. 40 minutes
700 kcal/2941 kJ*

Egg Noodles with Cocktail Shrimps and Snow Peas

Serves 4

9 oz/250 g Chinese egg noodles

salt

11 oz/300 g snow peas

1 bunch spring onions

2 small mild green chilies

2 tbsp sesame oil

9 oz/250 g cocktail shrimps

2 tbsp light soy sauce

2 tbsp sweet & sour chili sauce

6 eggs

Preparation time: ca. 35 minutes
562 kcal/2355 kJ

1   Cook the egg noodles in salted water according to the directions on the package. Nip off the ends of the snow peas, wash, dry and halve the pods. Wash and clean the spring onions and cut into fine rings. Wash and dry the chilies and cut into thin strips.

2   Heat the sesame oil in a wok and stir-fry the spring onions. First stir in the snow peas, followed by the chili strips. Finally add the noodles and stir-fry for another 3 minutes.

3   Add the shrimps and season with soy sauce and chili sauce. Push aside the noodle mixture in the wok and pour the whisked eggs into the middle. Scramble the eggs and then mix with the fried noodles.

70

Noodles with Pumpkin and Leaf Spinach in Soy Syrup

Serves 4

1 ¼ lb/600 g pumpkin

3 ½ oz/100 g fresh leaf spinach

9 oz/250 g broad rice noodles

4 tbsp vegetable oil

2 tbsp honey

8 tbsp soy sauce

2 tbsp sesame seeds

Preparation time: ca. 25 minutes
342 kcal/1431 kJ

1   Peel the pumpkin, remove the seeds and cut the flesh into strips. Clean the spinach, rinse thoroughly under running water and shake dry.

2   Cook the rice noodles in boiling water, stir to separate the noodles. Remove and rinse briefly with cold water.

3   Heat the oil in a wok and fry the pumpkin strips. Add the honey and soy sauce and cook until syrupy. Then add the cooked rice noodles and the spinach, mix carefully and heat up.

4   Cook until the spinach collapses. Serve sprinkled with sesame seeds.

Rice Vermicelli with Peppers, Garlic, and Coriander Salsa

1 Cook the rice vermicelli according to the directions on the package, pour off the liquid, rinse with cold water and allow to drain in a sieve.

2 Clean, wash, de-seed and dice the peppers. Cut the coriander leaves into thin strips.

3 Heat the oil in a wok, fry the pieces of pepper and the coriander leaves briefly at a high temperature. Do not overcook, the peppers should not be too soft.

4 Add the cooked rice vermicelli, pour in the fish sauce, honey and rice vinegar. Toss and serve immediately.

Serves 4

1 ¼ cups/250 g rice vermicelli

2 red and 2 yellow peppers

6 coriander leaves

4 tbsp vegetable oil

4 tbsp fish sauce

2 tbsp honey

2 tbsp rice vinegar

Preparation time: ca. 25 minutes
229 kcal/957 kJ

Serves 4

14 oz/400 g parsnips

½ bunch spring onions

11 oz/300 g snow peas

3–4 tbsp peanut oil

salt

pepper

nutmeg

mustard powder

3–4 tbsp maple syrup

2–3 tbsp Dijon mustard

peanut oil for deep-frying

4 ½ oz/125 g glass noodles

Preparation time: ca. 30 minutes
435 kcal/1828 kJ

Deep-fried Glass Noodles

1 Peel the parsnips and cut into small cubes. Clean the spring onions, wash and cut into pieces about ¾ to 2 in/ 2 to 5 cm long. Clean, wash and drain the snow peas.

2 Heat the oil in a wok and stir-fry the vegetables for about 3 to 4 minutes in batches. Season to taste with the spices, remove and allow to drain.

3 Stir the maple syrup and the mustard into the remaining cooking oil and heat gently. Return the vegetables and glaze. Take out and keep warm.

4 Clean the wok and heat enough peanut oil for deep-frying. Deep-fry the glass noodles in portions until crispy. Serve the vegetables together with the glass noodles.

Serves 4

½ cup/100 g brown rice

¼ cup/50 g small green puy lentils

2 cups/500 ml vegetable stock (ready-to-use)

salt

pepper

coriander and ginger powder

¼ cup/60 g pepper butter

3 ½ oz/100 g pearl onions in a jar

cumin and clove powder

1 tbsp raspberry vinegar

4–5 tbsp plain yogurt

*Preparation time: ca. 30 minutes
298 kcal/1253 kJ*

73

Yogurt Rice with Lentils

1 Cook the rice with the lentils in the vegetable stock for about 20 minutes. Season to taste with salt, pepper, coriander and ginger powder.

2 Heat the butter in a wok. Stir-fry the well-drained pearl onions for 4 to 5 minutes. Put the rice and lentil mixture in a sieve and allow to drain well. Add to the pearl onions.

3 Season to taste with cumin and clove powder. Add vinegar and cook at a moderate temperature for about 3 to 4 minutes. Fold in the yogurt carefully and serve immediately.

Poultry

Asia's most famous poultry dish is of course Peking Duck. This chapter is intended to show you how much more Asian cuisine has to offer. Enjoy the following wok recipes for chicken, turkey, duck, guinea fowl, goose or pheasant. Braised, deep-fried or marinated with seasoning pastes — the variety in cooking methods is only surpassed by the culinary enjoyment afterwards.

Guinea Fowl Sticks

Serves 4

1 ¼ lb/600 g guinea fowl breast fillets

3–4 tbsp lemon-pepper seasoning

generous 1 cup/150 g chickpea flour

2–3 tsp oil

1 tsp ground cumin

¼ tsp ground coriander

¼ tsp cayenne pepper

1 pinch of salt

peanut oil for deep-frying

1 bunch mint

1 bunch lemon balm

generous ¾ cup/200 g yogurt

2 tbsp heavy cream

pimento, mustard, and garlic powder

pepper

½ head of lollo rosso

Preparation time: ca. 30 minutes
716 kcal/3010 kJ

1 Cut the meat into thin strips. Season the strips of meat with lemon-pepper seasoning and allow to stand for about 10 to 15 minutes. Mix the flour with the oil, the spices and 3 ½ tbsp/50 ml of water. Heat sufficient peanut oil in a wok.

2 Cover the meat pieces with the batter and deep-fry in the peanut oil until golden brown. Wash, dry and finely chop the herbs. Mix the yogurt with the heavy cream until smooth. Fold in the herbs and season to taste with the pimento, garlic and powder, salt and pepper.

3 Wash and dry the salad, and line a large plate with the salad leaves. Put the yogurt dip in a small bowl and place in the middle of the plate. Surround with the pieces of meat and serve.

Turkey Ragout with Coconut

Serves 4

1 ¼ lb/600 g turkey breast fillets

1 red pepper

9 oz/250 g spring onions

1 bunch basil

1 ⅔ cups/400 ml unsweetened coconut milk

1 tbsp red curry paste

2 tbsp soy sauce

1 tbsp sugar

Preparation time: ca. 20 minutes
290 kcal/1221 kJ

1 Wash the turkey breast fillets, dry and cut into strips. Wash the pepper, halve, de-seed and cut into strips.

2 Clean and wash the spring onions and cut into 2 in/5 cm long pieces. Wash and dry the basil. Pluck the leaves from the stems and chop half of the leaves finely. Put aside the remaining leaves for garnishing.

3 Bring the coconut milk to the boil in the wok, add the meat and the curry paste and simmer for about 1 minute while stirring occasionally. Add the vegetables prepared earlier and simmer for another 3 minutes. Add the chopped basil, soy sauce and sugar, and season to taste.

Chicken Breast with Apricot Sauce

1   Cut the chicken breast into pieces of about ¾ in/2 cm. Peel and finely chop the ginger, the shallot and the garlic.

2   Mix half of the ginger with the garlic, sesame oil and 3 tablespoons of soy sauce. Clean and wash the lemon grass, finely chop and add .

3   Add the chicken and mix. Allow to marinate in the fridge while covered for at least 3 hours, if possible over night.

4   Mix the remaining ginger with the sambal oelek, the rest of the soy sauce and the lime juice. Clean and wash the spring onions, and cut into rings. Add the apricot jam with the spring onion rings and mix.

5   Heat the oil in a wok. Stir-fry the chicken until cooked, pouring some of the marinade over the almost done meat. Serve the meat with the sauce.

Serves 4

1 ½ lb/700 g chicken breast fillets

1 piece of fresh ginger (ca. 1 ¼ in/4 cm)

1 shallot

1 garlic clove

3 tbsp light sesame oil

6 tbsp light soy sauce

1 stalk lemon grass

½ tsp sambal oelek

2 tbsp lime juice

4 spring onions

4 tbsp apricot jam

2–3 tbsp oil for frying

Preparation time: ca. 30 minutes (plus marinating time)
245 kcal/1027 kJ

79

Chicken in Lemon Sauce

Serves 4

1 ½ lb/700 g chicken breast fillets

1 egg yolk

2 tsp soy sauce

2 tbsp dry sherry

5 ½ tbsp cornstarch

2 ½ tbsp flour

oil for deep-frying

⅓ cup/80 ml lemon juice

2 tbsp sugar

4 spring onions in bite-sized pieces

Preparation time: ca. 45 minutes
243 kcal/1021 kJ

1 Cut the chicken breast fillets into strips about ⅓ in/ 1 cm wide. Mix the egg yolk with 1 tablespoon of water, soy sauce, 1 tablespoon of sherry and 1 ½ tablespoons of cornstarch in a bowl until smooth. Pour the mixture over the meat, mix and allow to stand for 10 minutes.

2 Sieve 3 tablespoons of flour on to a plate, coat the strips of meat with the flour. Heat the oil in a wok and deep-fry the meat until golden brown. Remove and allow to drain on a paper towel, put aside.

3 Heat up the lemon juice with 2 tablespoons of water, sugar and the remaining sherry at a medium temperature, stirring until the sugar has dissolved. Mix the remaining cornstarch and one tablespoon of water to a smooth paste, add to thicken the sauce. Serve the meat sprinkled with the spring onions and the sauce.

Lemon Duck

Serves 4

3 tbsp honey

1 ½ tbsp aniseed

1 tsp soy sauce

1 tsp ground ginger

grated lemon peel and juice of 1 organic lemon

4 duck legs

pepper

salt

1–2 tbsp olive oil

1 fresh whole bulb of garlic

2 leeks

1 tbsp peeled almonds

2 tbsp butter

Preparation time: ca. 15 minutes (plus cooking and frying time)
463 kcal/1943 kJ

1 Cook the honey, aniseed, soy sauce, ginger, lemon peel and lemon juice for 10 minutes. Strain and cook until syrupy.

2 Salt and pepper the duck legs and fry slowly for 12 minutes in oil with the skin side down. Turn over the meat and continue frying for 10 minutes. Keep basting with marinade throughout frying.

3 Peel and halve the garlic cloves, clean the leek, wash and diagonally slice into ¾ in/2 cm thick pieces. Fry slowly with the garlic and almonds in butter for 10 minutes and serve with the duck legs.

Serves 4

1 cup/200 g basmati rice

4 duck breasts
(5 ½ oz/160 g each)

10–12 stalks lemon grass

5 garlic cloves

1 piece of fresh ginger
(about 1 in/3 cm)

scant 1 cup/225 ml hoisin
sauce

scant 1 cup/225 ml soy
sauce

4 tbsp sesame oil

3 ½ tbsp/50 ml rice wine

3–4 tbsp honey

1–2 tbsp mixed Chinese
spices

salt

pepper

¾ cup/125 g tempura flour

3 egg whites

2 small zucchini

oil for deep-frying

*Preparation time: ca. 20 minutes
(plus frying time)
610 kcal/2562 kJ*

Glazed Duck on Lemon Grass Skewer

1 Cook the rice according to the instructions on the package. Slice the duck breasts diagonally to obtain 3 to 4 similarly sized pieces. Clean and wash the lemon grass and use to skewer the duck breast pieces.

2 Preheat the oven to 390 °F/200 °C/gas 6. Peel the garlic and crush. Peel and finely chop the ginger. Mix the garlic, ginger, hoisin sauce, soy sauce, sesame oil, 2 ½ tbsp/40 ml rice wine, honey and mixed Chinese spices as marinade.

3 Salt and pepper the meat, first fry the skin side until crispy, turn over and fry for another minute. Then baste with the marinade. Roast in the oven for about 10 minutes. Baste with the marinade every 2 minutes.

4 Mix the tempura flour with water and the egg whites.

5 Clean and wash the zucchini and cut into slices about ⅕ in/½ cm thick. Heat the oil, cover the zucchini slices with the batter and deep-fry one after the other in the oil until golden brown. Take out and allow to drain on a paper towel.

6 Reduce the meat juices from roasting with the remaining marinade and rice wine, until a creamy sauce is obtained. Strain the sauce and pour over the duck breast skewers before serving.

Goose Breast with Chickpeas

Serves 4

11 oz/300 g chickpeas, canned

1 cup/200 g alfalfa sprouts

1 bunch spring onions

⅔ cup/100 g corn, canned

3–4 tbsp chili oil

½ bunch savory

½ cup/125 ml malt beer

coriander, clove and mustard powder

14 oz/400 g smoked goose breast

Preparation time: ca. 20 minutes
459 kcal/1930 kJ

1 Put the peas in a strainer and allow to drain well. Wash and dry the alfalfa sprouts.

2 Clean and wash the spring onions and cut into fine rings. Put the corn in a sieve and allow to drain well.

3 Heat the oil in a wok and stir-fry the vegetables for 4 to 5 minutes in portions.

4 Wash and dry the savory and pluck off the leaves. Add to the chickpeas together with the malt beer and cook at a moderate temperature for about 4 to 5 minutes.

5 Season the vegetables with coriander, cloves and mustard powder to taste. Cut the goose breast in thin slices and serve together with the chickpea vegetables and the alfalfa sprouts.

Goose Breast with Fruit

1 Cut the goose breast into strips. Clean the leek, wash and cut into thin rings. Peel the pomelos and grapefruit, removing the white skin. Then carefully remove the fillets.

2 First cut the guavas into wedges lengthways, peel and then cut into cubes. Wash and peel the kaffir lime, chopping the peel finely. Wash and finely chop the leaves as well. Clean, wash and finely chop the lemon grass.

3 Heat the oil in a wok and fry the meat. Add the pomelo, grapefruit, lime peel, lime leaves, guava and lemon grass after about 3 minutes. Season to taste with the spices. After about 8 minutes, serve garnished with the lime slices.

Serves 4

2 lb/900 g smoked goose breast

1 leek

2 pomelos

2 pink grapefruit

2 guavas

4 kaffir limes

2 kaffir lime leaves

1 stalk lemon grass

4 tbsp peanut oil

1 tsp each of aniseed, clove, and ginger powder

thin lime slices for garnishing

Preparation time: ca. 30 minutes
789 kcal/3315 kJ

Serves 4

12 chicken wings

salt

pepper

3 tbsp sesame oil

4–5 tbsp liquid honey

5 tbsp vegetable oil

1 orange

1 ½ tbsp sugar

Preparation time: ca. 40 minutes
(plus marinating time)
398 kcal/1670 kJ

Chicken Wings with Orange Sauce

1   Season the chicken wings with salt and pepper. Mix the sesame oil with the honey, carefully coating the chicken wings. Allow to stand for 30 minutes.

2   Heat the vegetable oil in a wok and fry the chicken wings at a high temperature for 4 minutes on each side until they are almost done.

3   Remove the wok from the heat, take out the chicken wings and keep warm. Wash the orange with hot water, rub dry, grate the peel and remove some fine shreds of zest. Finally squeeze the orange.

4   Heat the sugar very slowly without stirring until it caramelizes; remove from the heat. Add the orange juice and the meat juices from frying. Stir at a low temperature until a smooth sauce is obtained. Add some more water or orange juice if necessary.

5   Add half of the grated orange peel and allow to simmer gently for 3 minutes. Serve the chicken wings with the orange sauce poured over them and sprinkled with the remaining orange zest.

Chicken in Ginger Wine

Serves 4

14 oz/400 g chicken breast fillets

1 piece of fresh ginger (1 ¼ in/3 cm)

3 garlic cloves

3–4 tbsp sesame oil

salt

pepper

ginger and coriander powder

3 tbsp spicy ketchup

2 ½ tbsp/40 ml dry sherry

4 tsp/20 ml plum wine

½ bunch coriander

Tabasco sauce

Preparation time: ca. 20 minutes
397 kcal/1668 kJ

1 Wash the chicken breast fillets, dry and cut into thin strips. Peel the ginger and grate finely. Peel and dice the garlic cloves.

2 Heat the oil in a wok and stir-fry the strips of meat with the ginger and the diced garlic for 5 to 6 minutes. Season with salt, pepper, ginger and coriander powder.

3 Put ketchup, sherry and plum wine in the wok and cook at a moderate temperature for another 3 to 5 minutes. Wash and dry the coriander and remove the leaves.

4 Season the chicken with Tabasco sauce and serve garnished with coriander. Goes well with prawn crackers.

Curry with Turkey and Chili

1   Wash the chilies and the peppers, halve lengthwise, de-seed and cut into strips. Wash and dry the meat and also cut into strips. Heat the oil and braise the meat.

2   Add the vegetables. Stir in the five-spice powder and the curry paste. Then pour in the stock. Stir in the fish sauce and the soy sauce.

3   Wash, dry and finely chop the kaffir lime leaves and add together with the lemon juice. Allow to simmer at a moderate temperature for about 10 minutes. Serve with basmati rice.

Serves 4

6 mild green chilies

3 red chilies

1 yellow pepper

1 red pepper

1 turkey breast fillet

4 tbsp sesame oil

1 tbsp chili oil

2 tbsp five-spice powder

3 tbsp green curry paste (ready-to-use)

2 cups/500 ml chicken/turkey stock

1 cup/250 ml Asian-style stock

3 tbsp fish sauce (ready-to-use)

3 tbsp light soy sauce

2 kaffir lime leaves

1 tbsp lemon juice

Preparation time: ca. 35 minutes
571 kcal/2401 kJ

Chicken Breast Fillet with Tofu and Vegetables

1   Wash the chicken breast fillets, dry and cut into thin strips. Peel and finely dice the shallots.

2   Put the pumpkin, the baby corn-on-the-cobs and the celery in a strainer and allow to drain well. Chop everything into thin strips. Mix the strips of meat with the vegetables.

3   Mix the oil with the hoisin sauce and the rice wine, pour over the meat and vegetable mixture and allow to marinate for about 15 minutes. Then braise with the marinade in the wok for 8 to 10 minutes.

4   Cut the tofu into cubes and add carefully. Season well with the five-spice powder and serve in small bowls.

Serves 4

11 oz/300 g chicken breast fillet

2 shallots

3 ½ oz/100 g pickled pumpkin

3 ½ oz/100 g baby corn-on-the-cob, canned

3 ½ oz/100 g celeriac

2–3 tbsp sesame oil

3–4 tbsp hoisin sauce (ready-to-use)

3–4 tbsp rice wine

3 ½ oz/100 g tofu

five-spice powder

Preparation time: ca. 40 minutes
324 kcal/1363 kJ

Serves 4

**4 chicken drumsticks
(7 oz/200 g each)**

**7 oz/200 g large field
mushrooms**

3 ½ oz/100 g fennel

3 ½ oz/100 g snow peas

3 ½ oz/100 g parsnips

salt

pepper

paprika powder

mustard powder

**2–3 tbsp peanut or sesame
oil**

*Preparation time: ca. 30 minutes
625 kcal/2625 kJ*

Spicy Chicken Drumsticks

1 Wash and dry the chicken drumsticks, and cut the skin crosswise. Clean the mushrooms and slice. Clean, wash and slice the fennel. Put aside the green herb tops for garnishing.

2 Nip off the tips of the snow peas and wash. Peel the parsnips and slice.

3 Rub the drumsticks well with the spices and fry in the oil on all sides.

4 Put the vegetables in a bamboo basket. Place the drumsticks on top and steam the contents for 15 to 20 minutes in the wok.

5 Serve the chicken drumsticks with the vegetables garnished with the fennel sprigs.

Crispy Duck with Pineapple

1 Mix the flour with the oil, milk, eggs, salt, port and desiccated coconut to a smooth batter. Peel and quarter the baby pineapples and remove the stalks.

2 Wash the duck fillet, dry and cut into cubes. Heat up sufficient peanut oil in a wok. Coat the meat cubes and pineapple quarters with the batter and deep-fry for about 6 to 8 minutes in portions. Remove and allow to drain on a paper towel and keep warm.

3 For the red dip, allow the mandarins and ginger to drain in a strainer. Season with ketchup, coriander, clove and aniseed powder and cayenne pepper. Purée using a blender.

4 For the yellow dip, mix the mayonnaise with the yogurt until smooth. Peel the apple and the banana and cut into small cubes. Add to the yogurt mayonnaise, together with the curry powder, the almonds and the maple syrup. Stir well and add salt to taste.

5 Wash and dry the lemon balm and remove the leaves. Wash the lemon and slice. Serve the two dips with the meat and pineapple pieces, garnished with slices of lemon and lemon balm.

Serves 4

generous 1 ¼ cups/180–200 g wholewheat flour

1 tbsp walnut oil

4–5 tbsp milk

2–3 eggs

1 pinch of salt

½ cup/125 ml port

generous 1 cup/100 g shredded coconut

2 baby pineapples

1 ¾ lb/800 g duck breast filets

peanut oil for deep-frying

1 ½ cups/150 g mandarin oranges, canned

5 oz/150 g sweet & sour pickled ginger (ready-to-use)

2–3 tbsp ketchup

coriander, clove, and aniseed powder

cayenne pepper

10 tbsp/150 g mayonnaise

6 tbsp/100 g yogurt

1 small apple

1 banana

2 tbsp curry powder

1 tbsp chopped almonds

1 tbsp maple syrup

½ bunch lemon balm

1 organic lemon

Preparation time: ca. 30 minutes
1394 kcal/5869 kJ

Meat

Very hot or sweet and sour: the wok is simply excellent for sumptuous meat dishes. The typical style of cooking for a short time yet at high temperatures leaves the meat crispy and crunchy outside while remaining tender and succulent inside. Discover some Asian specialties with pork, beef, lamb and game, each complemented perfectly by selected spices, herbs and vegetables.

Szechuan Style Beef

1 Cut the beef into thin slices. Mix the egg white with the cornstarch and 1 tablespoon of soy sauce and marinate the beef in this mixture.

2 Peel the onions and the garlic, cutting the onions in fine rings. Clean, wash and finely chop the peppers and the chilies. Clean and wash the leek and cut into thin strips. Clean, wash and dice the eggplant. Peel and chop the ginger.

3 Mix the sugar with the remaining soy sauce, rice vinegar and rice wine and put aside.

4 Heat the oil in a wok. Stir-fry the beef at a high temperature. Season with salt and pepper. Take out and put aside.

5 Heat some oil and fry the eggplants, onions, ginger and the rest of the vegetables. Add the pressed garlic. Stir-fry at a high temperature. Add the meat. Pour in the sauce and mix all of the ingredients well. Goes well with rice.

Serves 4

generous 1 lb/500 g beef

1 egg white

1 tbsp cornstarch

4 tbsp soy sauce

2 onions

2 garlic cloves

1 red and 1 green pepper

2 chilies

1 small leek

1 small eggplant

**1 piece of fresh ginger
(ca. 1 ¼ in/3 cm)**

1 tsp sugar

1 tsp rice vinegar

2 tbsp rice wine

oil for frying

1 pinch of salt

pepper

*Preparation time: ca. 20 minutes
(plus frying time)
278 kcal/1165 kJ*

93

Spicy Fried Pepper Beef

Serves 4

1 ¼ lb/600 g rump steak

4–5 tbsp sesame oil

1 ¾ oz/50 g pickled green peppercorns

1 cup/100 g mandarin oranges

salt

½ bunch chives

Preparation time: ca. 20 minutes
449 kcal/1886 kJ

1   Cut the meat into thin strips. Heat the oil in a wok and stir-fry the strips of meat for about 3 to 4 minutes.

2   Drain the peppercorns well and add. Put the mandarins in a strainer and also drain well. Collect the liquid.

3   Put the mandarins in the wok and braise for about 1 to 2 minutes. Add 2 to 3 tablespoons of the collected mandarin liquid and add salt to taste.

4   Wash, dry and finely chop the chives. Serve the peppery meat sprinkled with chives.

Beef Fillet in Mussaman Curry

Serves 4

generous 1 lb/500 g fillet of beef

2 tbsp oil

4 tbsp mussaman curry paste

1 quart/1 l coconut milk

generous 1 lb/500 g potatoes, diced

1 chopped onion

½ cup/75 g unsalted peanuts

1 stick of cinnamon

several cardamom seeds

3 tbsp fish sauce

3 tbsp tamarind juice

2 tbsp palm sugar

Preparation time: ca. 15 minutes
(plus cooking time)
335 kcal/1407 kJ

1   Cut the meat into slices. Heat the oil in a wok. Add curry paste and stir-fry until a pleasant smell is developed.

2   Add the coconut milk while stirring and heat. Add the potato cubes, onions, peanuts, cinnamon and cardamoms to the wok and allow to simmer for 20 minutes with the lid on.

3   Add the meat and allow to cook gently for 10 minutes. Season to taste with fish sauce, tamarind juice and palm sugar. Serve as soon as the potatoes and the meat are cooked.

Sour Lamb Strips

1 Wash the meat, dry and cut into thin strips. Mix the oil with the spices and allow the strips of meat to marinate in the mixture for about 15 to 20 minutes.

2 Put the strips of meat and the marinade in a hot wok and stir-fry for about 5 to 6 minutes.

3 Add the mixed pickles with the liquid and braise for 3 to 4 minutes. Stir in the sour cream, and serve the strips of meat and the vegetables in small bowls.

Serves 4

generous 1 lb/500 g fillet of lamb

2–3 tbsp sesame oil

salt

pepper

garlic, ginger and cardamom powder

1 pinch of rosemary powder

9 oz/250 g mixed pickles

1–2 tbsp sour cream

Preparation time: ca. 40 minutes
267 kcal/1121 kJ

Spicy Fried Meat

Serves 4

2 ¼ lb/1 kg lean pork

12 garlic cloves

2 shallots

1 ½ tsp freshly ground black pepper

3 tbsp fish sauce (ready-to-use)

2 tbsp red wine vinegar

1 tbsp light soy sauce

1 tbsp dark soy sauce

1 tbsp yellow curry paste (ready-to-use)

1 tbsp chili sauce (ready-to-use)

5 tbsp sunflower oil

1 bitter cucumber

3 ½ oz/100 g stoned black olives

2 tbsp sesame seeds

freshly grated nutmeg

Preparation time: ca. 40 minutes (plus marinating time)
634 kcal/2665 kJ

1 Cut the meat into 1 ½ in/4 cm long and ¾ in/2 cm wide strips and put in a bowl. Peel and finely slice the garlic. Peel the shallots and dice. Mix the shallots and the meat with the pepper, fish sauce, red wine vinegar, soy sauce, curry paste and chili sauce. Pour the sauce over the meat, cover and allow to marinate for about 1 hour.

2 Wash the cucumber, halve lengthways and cut into slices. Drain the olives and cut in half. Heat the oil in a wok and fry the meat. Add the bitter cucumber, olives and sesame seeds. Season to taste with nutmeg and allow to simmer for another 7 minutes. Serve on plates.

Hot Curry

Serves 4

1 ¼ lb/600 g boned pork chop

5–6 tbsp sesame oil

1 onion, chopped

1 or 2 cloves garlic, minced

½ cup/125 ml vegetable stock

1 tbsp plum sauce (ready-to-use)

2 tbsp green curry paste

1–2 tbsp pine nuts

Preparation time: ca. 20 minutes
360 kcal/1513 kJ

1 Cut the meat into small cubes. Heat the oil in a wok and stir-fry the meat at a high temperature. Take out and keep warm.

2 Put the onion, cloves garlic, vegetable stock, plum sauce and curry paste in the oil left from frying and simmer for about 2 to 3 minutes at a moderate temperature. Add the meat and braise for about 6 to 7 minutes. Serve the curry sprinkled with the roasted pine kernels.

Venison with Plums

1   Cut the meat into thin slices. Heat the oil in a wok and stir-fry the slices for about 3 to 4 minutes.

2   Put the plums in a strainer and drain well. Add to the meat and pour in the game stock.

3   Add the plum jam, dark beer and vinegar and braise for about 6 to 8 minutes. Season well to taste with salt, cayenne pepper, ginger, clove and coriander powder.

4   Wash, dry and finely chop the coriander leaves. Serve the meat sprinkled with the coriander leaves.

Serves 4

14 oz/400 g venison fillet

4–5 tbsp sesame oil

5 oz/150 g plums in a jar

½ cup/125 ml game stock (ready-to-use)

3–4 tbsp plum jam

3–4 tbsp dark beer

1 tbsp red wine vinegar

salt

cayenne pepper

ginger, clove and coriander powder

½ bunch coriander

Preparation time: ca. 20 minutes
295 kcal/1241 kJ

Hare Fillet with Grapes

1   Wash the grapes, halve and remove the seeds. Mix the grapes with the raisins, the armagnac and the five-spice powder and marinate for about 10 to 15 minutes.

2   Cut the hare fillet into thin strips. Heat the oil in a wok and stir-fry the strips of meat with the diced bacon for about 3 to 4 minutes.

3   Add the grape mixture and braise for about 3 to 4 minutes. Season well with salt and pepper. Wash the lentil sprouts, drain and add. Heat for about 1 to 2 minutes while stirring and serve.

Serves 4

11 oz/300 g white grapes

6 tbsp/50 g raisins

2 ½ tbsp/40 ml armagnac

½ tbsp five-spice powder

generous 1 lb/500 g hare fillet

2–3 tbsp sesame oil

3 ½ oz/100 g diced bacon

salt

pepper

3 ½ oz/100 g lentil sprouts

Preparation time: ca. 30 minutes
347 kcal/1459 kJ

Stuffed Meat Roulades

Serves 4

3 ½ oz/100 g boiled ham

1 onion, chopped

2 cloves garlic, minced

1 cup/100 g chopped mixed herbs

3 ½ oz/100 g shiitake mushrooms

3 ½ oz/100 g feta cheese

2–3 tbsp sesame oil

salt

pepper

14 oz/400 g very thin veal or pork escalopes

2–3 tbsp horseradish cream sauce

4–5 tbsp peanut oil

1–2 cups/250–500 ml Asian-style stock (ready-to-use)

hoisin sauce (ready-to-use) as a dip

Preparation time: ca. 40 minutes
508 kcal/2136 kJ

1 Cut the ham into small cubes and mix with the onion and cloves garlic.

2 Clean the mushrooms and cut into small cubes. Crumble the feta cheese and mix with the sesame oil, mushrooms and ham cubes. Season the mixture with salt and pepper.

3 Halve the escalopes lengthways. Spread on a work surface and coat with a thin layer of horseradish.

4 Put a layer of the ham mixture on top and roll up the escalopes. Secure with a small wooden skewer.

5 Heat the oil in a wok and fry the roulades on all sides at a high temperature. Take out the roulades and clean the wok.

6 Put the Asian-style stock in the wok and heat. Place the roulades in a bamboo basket. Put the basket in the wok, cover with a lid and steam the roulades in the stock for about 15 to 20 minutes. Serve the meat roulades with hoisin sauce.

Steamed Stuffed Cabbage

1 Clean the savoy cabbage leaves and blanch for 1 to 2 minutes in an adequate amount of boiling salted water. Remove, rinse with cold water and dry.

2 Wash, dry and finely chop the parsley. Also finely chop the capers. Work the parsley, capers, egg, oregano, caraway seeds, onion and garlic powder and ground pork into a smooth mixture, kneading well. Season with salt and pepper and spread on the cabbage leaves.

3 Fold in the sides of the leaves and roll up. Secure the roulades with small wooden skewers. Bring salted water to the boil in a wok and put the cabbage packages in a bamboo basket.

4 Place the basket in the wok and steam for 10 to 15 minutes with the lid on. Carefully lift out the cabbage roulades and serve.

Serves 4

8–10 medium size savoy cabbage leaves

salt

1 bunch parsley

1 tbsp capers

1 egg

1–2 tbsp oregano flakes

1 tbsp caraway seeds

onion and garlic powder

14 oz/400 g ground pork

cayenne pepper

Preparation time: ca. 30 minutes
376 kcal/1581 kJ

Serves 4

1 ¼ lb/600 g pork fillet

4 tbsp fish sauce

4 tbsp oyster sauce

4 limes

1 bunch coriander

4 tsp red peppercorns

*Preparation time: ca. 25 minutes
(plus 10 minutes marinating time)
205 kcal/858 kJ*

Steamed Pork Fillet with Coriander and Lime

1 Cut the meat into pieces of about ¾ in/2 cm. Marinate in fish and oyster sauce for 10 minutes. Slice the limes. Wash the coriander, shake dry and remove the leaves.

2 Line four bamboo baskets with the lime slices, put the marinated meat on top and sprinkle with coriander leaves. Cover the baskets with a lid.

3 Heat some water in a wok and place the baskets over the water. After 5 minutes, exchange the uppermost basket with the bottom basket to make sure the food is steamed evenly.

4 Allow the steamed meat to stand uncovered for another 6 to 8 minutes and then serve sprinkled with red peppercorns.

Steamed Stuffed Swiss Chard

1 Wash the leaves of the Swiss chard and blanch briefly. Cut 1 stalk of lemon grass in pieces, finely chopping one of the pieces with the peeled garlic. Soak the bread roll, peel the galangal and chop.

2 Mix the ground pork with the eggs, squeezed bread roll, finely chopped lemon grass and finely chopped garlic as well as the hoisin sauce and the ginger.

3 Spread the filling on the blanched Swiss chard leaves and form into little balls. Line the bamboo baskets with pieces of galangal root and lemon grass, place the Swiss chard packages on top and sprinkle with coriander oil.

4 Heat some water in a wok, place the bamboo baskets over it and steam for about 30 minutes with the lid on.

Serves 4

20 large leaves of Swiss chard

2 stalks lemon grass

1 garlic clove

1 bread roll

3 ½ oz/100 g galangal

generous 1 lb/500 g ground pork

3 eggs

1 tbsp hoisin sauce

1 tsp finely grated ginger

some coriander oil

Preparation time: ca. 50 minutes
376 kcal/1576 kJ

103

Serves 4

1 tsp saffron threads

1 ¼ cups/250 g basmati rice

2 onions

2 garlic cloves

1 piece of fresh ginger (ca. ¾ in/2 cm)

1 ¼ lb/600 g boneless lamb

salt

2 cloves

½ tsp black peppercorns

2 green cardamom capsules

1 tsp cumin seeds

¾ in/2 cm cinnamon stick

2 tbsp ghee or clarified butter

nutmeg

chili powder

generous ⅔ cups/180 g plain yogurt

4 tbsp raisins

4 tbsp roasted almond flakes

Preparation time: ca. 40 minutes (plus frying and cooking time)
580 kcal/2436 kJ

Lamb Biryani

1   Soak the saffron in lukewarm water and put aside. Wash the basmati rice and soak in cold water for 30 minutes.

2   Peel the onions and garlic and cut the onions into fine slices. Peel the ginger and grate. Cut the lamb into bite-sized pieces.

3   Heat some salted water, briefly allow the rice to come to the boil and cook very gently for 15 minutes at minimum heat. Finely grind the garlic, ginger, cloves, pepper, cardamom, cumin and cinnamon in a mortar.

4   Fry the onions in the fat until golden brown. Heat the mixed spices, a little freshly grated nutmeg and the chili powder for 1 minute while stirring. Add the lamb and fry evenly on all sides.

5   Stir in the yogurt with the raisins and the saffron liquid, heat and cook for about 40 minutes.

6   Arrange a pyramid of rice on a plate, sprinkle with the roasted almonds and serve with the meat biryani.

Spicy Lamb with Green Pepper and Bell Peppers

Serves 4

generous 1 lb/500 g leg of lamb

2 each yellow, green and red bell peppers

10 large pepper leaves

4 tbsp vegetable oil

1 tsp curry powder

1 tbsp five-spice powder

2 tbsp green peppercorns

Preparation time: ca. 25 minutes
435 kcal/1822 kJ

1 Cut the lamb into small cubes. Wash, dry and de-seed the peppers, and cut into diamond shapes. Cut 2 pepper leaves into very fine strips.

2 Heat the oil in a wok and sear the lamb cubes. Dust with curry and five-spice powder and remove.

3 Fry the peppers from all sides in the wok at a high temperature, then pour in generous ¾ cup/200 ml of water. Add the peppercorns and reduce almost completely. Add the fried pieces of lamb and stir in the pepper leaf strips. Line each plate with 2 pepper leaves and serve the meat on the green leaves.

Saddle of Lamb with Spinach and Cumin

Serves 4

generous 1 lb/500 g saddle of lamb

1 tsp curry powder

1 tsp cumin

1 tsp coriander seeds

3 shallots

2 garlic cloves

14 oz/400 g fresh leaf spinach

4 tbsp vegetable oil

½ tsp chili flakes

1 tsp hoisin sauce

Preparation time: ca. 25 minutes
594 kcal/2487 kJ

1 Cut the lamb into thin slices. Mix with curry, cumin and crushed coriander seeds.

2 Peel the shallots and cut into thin strips, peel and finely chop the garlic. Clean, wash and shake the spinach dry.

3 Heat the oil in a wok and sear the shallots and the garlic. Add the chili flakes, followed by the meat and the hoisin sauce and fry at a high temperature. Add the spinach and allow to collapse. Pour in some water and stir gently.

Beef with Spinach and Mango

1 Cut the meat into strips. Rinse the spinach thoroughly under running water, shake dry and chop roughly. Peel the mango and cut the flesh into diamond shapes. Wash the chilies and chop.

2 Heat the oil in a wok, sear the spinach and the chopped chilies, and remove. Use the same oil for frying the strips of meat at a high temperature. Pour in the soy and oyster sauce and stir well.

3 Add the mango pieces to the meat. Finally return the spinach and the chilies and mix with the meat. Season to taste with sweet and sour sauce and serve sprinkled with some Thai basil leaves.

Serves 4

generous 1 lb/500 g beef

7 oz/200 g leaf spinach

1 ripe mango

2 mild green chilies

3 tbsp vegetable oil

2 tbsp soy sauce

2 tbsp oyster sauce

3 tbsp sweet & sour sauce (ready-to-use)

½ bunch Thai basil

Preparation time: ca. 30 minutes
460 kcal/1925 kJ

107

Chop Suey

1 Soak the dried morels in hot water for at least 30 minutes. Cut the pork into pieces and mix with 1 pinch of salt, 1 tablespoon of soy sauce and the cornstarch.

2 Peel and roughly dice the onion. Drain the bamboo shoots and cut into strips. Drain the mung beans.

3 Clean, wash and halve the bell pepper, remove the base of the stalk and the seeds, and chop. Rinse and drain the mushrooms. Clean, wash and slice the leek.

4 Heat the oil, braise the onions and fry the pieces of meat. Add the rest of the soy sauce and the rice wine and braise for 4 minutes. Remove and keep warm.

5 Heat up the oil again and stir-fry the mung beans, pieces of pepper, leek rings, bamboo strips and morels for 3 to 4 minutes. Season to taste with pepper and sugar. Serve the meat together with the vegetables.

Serves 4

12 dried morels

generous 1 lb/500 g pork

salt

2 tbsp soy sauce

2 tsp cornstarch

1 onion

7 oz/200 g bamboo shoots in a jar

7 oz/200 g mung beans in a jar

1 red bell pepper

1 leek

oil for frying

3 tbsp rice wine

black pepper

1 tsp sugar

Preparation time: ca. 45 minutes (plus soaking time)
373 kcal/1565 kJ

109

Serves 4

14 oz/400 g pork escalopes

salt

pepper

flour

3–4 tbsp peanut oil

1 tbsp chili oil

generous 1 lb/500 g Swiss
chard

3 shallots

½ cup/125 ml veal stock
(ready-to-use)

3 ½ oz/100 g Parma ham

7 tbsp/50 g slivered
almonds

Preparation time: ca. 30 minutes
369 kcal/1550 kJ

Pork with Swiss Chard

1 Cut the escalopes into strips. Turn over in some salted and peppered flour. Heat both oils in a wok and stir-fry the strips of meat for about 4 to 5 minutes. Take out and keep warm.

2 Clean, wash, dry and finely chop the Swiss chard. Peel and finely chop the shallots. Fry the diced shallots and the Swiss chard in the oil left from frying the meat for 2 to 3 minutes.

3 Pour in the veal stock and simmer at a moderate temperature for 4 to 5 minutes. Cut the ham into thin strips and add together with the meat.

4 Roast the almond slivers in a pan without any oil. Serve sprinkled with the almond slivers.

Braised Shoulder

1 Cut the meat into small pieces. Heat the oil a wok and fry the pieces of meat for 4 to 5 minutes.

2 Mix the vinegar with the soy sauce, honey, spice powder and veal stock. Add to the meat, together with the vegetables and herbs for making a soup (normally pieces of carrot, celery, leek and parsley) and the pearl onions and braise for about 15 to 20 minutes while stirring.

3 Add some soy sauce to taste. Remove the meat and keep warm. Mix the cornstarch with some cold water and use to thicken the stock.

4 Serve the vegetables with the meat and the mango chutney.

Serves 4

1 ½ lb/650 g pork shoulder

3–4 tbsp sesame oil

3 tbsp sherry vinegar

6 tbsp soy sauce

4 tbsp honey

1 tbsp five-spice powder

½–1 cup/125–250 ml veal stock (ready-to-use)

3 ½ oz/100 g herbs and vegetables for making soup (fresh or dried)

3 ½ oz/100 g pickled pearl onions

1 tsp cornstarch

mango chutney (ready-to-use) for serving

Preparation time: ca. 35 minutes
674 kcal/2830 kJ

111

Asian Goulash

1 Cut the meat into similarly sized small cubes. Peel and finely dice the onions and garlic cloves.

2 Fry the diced onions and garlic with the herbs and vegetables for making a soup (normally pieces of carrot, celery, leek and parsley) in the peanut oil for 2 to 3 minutes. Add the meat and stir-fry for about 3 to 4 minutes.

3 Put the lentils in a strainer and allow to drain well. Add to the meat in the wok, together with the Asian-style stock and allow to simmer at a moderate temperature for about 4 to 5 minutes.

4 Season the goulash appropriately with soy sauce, vinegar and spices. Wash, dry and finely chop the coriander. Serve the goulash sprinkled with coriander.

Serves 4

1 ¼ lb/600 g pork

2–3 red onions

2 garlic cloves

3 ½ oz/100 g herbs and vegetables for making soup (fresh or dried)

4–5 tbsp peanut oil

11–14 oz/300–400 g lentils, canned

½ cup/125 ml Asian-style stock (ready-to-use)

1–2 tbsp soy sauce

1–2 tbsp cider vinegar

salt

pepper

clove powder

1 pinch of sugar

½ bunch coriander

Preparation time: ca. 20 minutes
589 kcal/2474 kJ

Mongolian Fillet of Lamb

1　Slice the lamb, cutting across the grain. Peel the garlic, ginger and onions. Quarter the onions, finely chop the garlic and ginger. Mix with the hoisin sauce and the sesame oil. Coat the meat evenly, cover and allow to marinate in the fridge for 60 minutes.

2　Roast the sesame seeds in a pan without any oil for 3 minutes at medium heat while stirring constantly until golden brown. Remove to prevent the seeds from getting burnt.

3　Heat the peanut oil in a wok and stir-fry the quartered onions at a medium temperature for 10 minutes until golden brown. Take out and keep warm.

4　Heat the wok again and sear the meat in portions at a high temperature. Finally return all of the meat to the wok. Cut the spring onions into rings.

5　Mix the cornstarch with the soy sauce and rice wine until smooth and add. Continue to stir-fry the meat at a high temperature until it is done and the sauce thickens. Serve the meat on a bed of onions, sprinkled with spring onions and roasted sesame seeds.

Serves 4

2 ¼ lb/1 kg lamb
3 garlic cloves
1 piece of fresh ginger (ca. 2 ¾ in/7 cm)
4 large onions
1 tbsp hoisin sauce
1 tbsp sesame oil
2 tbsp sesame seeds
2 tbsp peanut oil
½ bunch spring onions
3 tsp cornstarch
3 tbsp soy sauce
3 ¼ cups/750 ml rice wine

Preparation time: ca. 40 minutes (plus marinating time)
438 kcal/1838 kJ

Serves 4

1 ¼ lb/600 g venison goulash

3–4 tbsp raspberry vinegar

4–5 tbsp red wine

1 tsp hot Chinese mustard

5–6 tbsp sesame oil

salt

pepper

cloves, aniseed and cardamom powder

11 oz/300 g beet strips in a jar

7 oz/200 g red onions

Preparation time: ca. 40 minutes (plus marinating time)
350 kcal/1473 kJ

Hot and Sour Venison

1 Cut the goulash into smaller cubes if necessary. Mix the vinegar with the red wine, mustard, oil and spices, pour over the meat and allow to marinate for about 10 to 15 minutes.

2 Heat the wok and stir-fry the meat with the marinade for about 10 to 15 minutes.

3 Put the beet in a strainer and drain well. Peel the onions and cut into rings. Add these two ingredients to the goulash 5 minutes before the end of the cooking time. Serve the goulash with wild rice.

114

Spicy Stuffed Rotis

1 Mix the flour with a tablespoon of salt. Rub 2 tablespoons of ghee over the mixture. Mix the egg with 1 cup/250 ml of water, add and work the ingredients into a moist mixture. Place on a work surface dusted with flour and knead the dough for 10 minutes. Brush with oil and allow to rest for at least 2 hours, wrapped in cling film.

2 Heat the remaining ghee. Braise the shallots for 5 minutes. Peel and press the garlic and add together with the cumin and turmeric, braising for 1 minute. Add the mince and stir-fry. Add the chilies and season with salt to taste.

3 Divide the dough into 12 portions and roll into small balls. With slightly oily fingertips, pull the edges of the dough balls outwards to make circular sheets of pastry about 6 in/15 cm in diameter and cover with cling film. Whisk the egg.

4 Coat the wok with oil, carefully placing one flat bread in the wok. Brush with egg, put 2 heaped tablespoons of the stuffing on top and fry until the underside of the roti has a golden color.

5 Fold the roti in half, pressing the edges together a little, and keep warm. Fry the remaining rotis in a similar manner. Keep warm.

Serves 4

13 oz/375 g roti or
2 ½ cups/375 g flour

salt

3 tbsp ghee

1 egg

oil

2 chopped shallots

3 garlic cloves

2 tsp ground cumin

1 tsp ground turmeric

generous 1 lb/500 g lean
ground beef or lamb

3 finely chopped red chilies

oil or ghee for frying

*Preparation time: ca. 50 minutes
(plus resting time)
603 kcal/2530 kJ*

Fish

The Asian countries are surrounded by the sea, which is reflected by the traditional importance of fish dishes in Asian cuisine. Deep-fried, braised or steamed, as fish balls, fillet or curry: wok cooking has a lot to offer fish lovers who appreciate a variety of tasty, light food.

Steamed Carp

Serves 4

2 ¼– 3 ¼ lb/ 1–1 ½ kg carp fillets

2–3 tbsp rice wine or dry sherry

2–3 tbsp sea salt

2–3 tbsp pepper

4 shallots

1 piece of fresh ginger (1 ¼ in/3 cm)

2 red bell peppers

3 ½ oz/100 g bamboo shoots, canned

5–6 tbsp soy sauce

2 cups/500 ml fish stock (ready-to-use)

2–3 tbsp Chinese mustard

1 tbsp cornstarch

2–3 tbsp sour cream

Preparation time: ca. 40 minutes
409 kcal/1720 kJ

1   Wash and dry the pieces of fish and sprinkle with rice wine. Rub with salt and pepper and place into steamer baskets. Peel and quarter the shallots. Peel and slice the ginger. Halve and de-seed the peppers, wash and cut into diamond shapes.

2   Put the bamboo shoots in a strainer and drain well. Mix the vegetables and sprinkle with soy sauce. Distribute the mixed vegetables over the carp pieces. Bring the fish stock to the boil in a wok. Place the steamer basket inside and steam for about 15 to 20 minutes at a moderate temperature.

3   Remove the basket and stir the mustard into about 1 ½ cup/350 ml fish stock. Mix the cornstarch with some cold water and use to thicken the fish stock. Season the sauce to taste and improve with sour cream.

4   Serve the pieces of carp together with the vegetables and the sauce.

Sea Bass Roulades

Serves 4

1 zucchini

2 thin leeks

3 tomatoes

3 carrots

7 oz/200 g large field mushrooms

3 ½ oz/100 g boiled ham

1 tbsp five-spice powder

3–4 tbsp sesame oil

4 sea bass fillets (7 oz/200 g each)

1–2 tbsp wasabi

2–3 ¼ cups/500-750 ml fish stock (ready-to-use)

2–3 tbsp soy sauce

Preparation time: ca. 35 minutes
328 kcal/1379 kJ

1   Clean, wash and finely dice the zucchini and leeks. Skin the tomatoes, de-seed and dice. Peel and dice the carrots. Clean and chop the mushrooms.

2   Cut the ham into thin strips. Season the vegetables with five-spice powder. Heat the oil in a wok and stir-fry the vegetables with the ham for 4 to 5 minutes.

3   Wash and dry the fish fillets. Diagonally slice into thin pieces. Spread a thin layer of wasabi on the slices, followed by a topping of the vegetable and ham mixture. Roll up and secure with small wooden skewers.

4   Heat the fish stock and soy sauce in a wok. Put the fish roulades in a bamboo basket. Place this in a wok and steam the fish at a moderate temperature for about 4 to 5 minutes. Serve the fish roulades with basmati rice.

Braised Eel with Fennel

Serves 4

1 ¾ lb/800 g eel

4–5 tbsp sherry vinegar

1 tbsp coarse sea salt

1 ¾ oz/50 g pickled ginger

7 oz/200 g parsnips

11 oz/300 g fennel

6–7 tbsp sesame oil

1 tbsp fennel seeds

salt

cayenne pepper

½–1 cup/125–250 ml fish
stock (ready-to-use)

½ bunch parsley

lemon zest for garnishing

Preparation time: ca. 35 minutes
(plus marinating time)
293 kcal/1232 kJ

1 Wash the eel and cut into pieces about 1 ¼ to 1 ½ in/ 3 to 4 cm wide. Sprinkle with vinegar and sea salt. Allow to stand for approximately 5 to 8 minutes.

2 Put the ginger in a strainer and drain well. Clean, wash and chop the parsnips and the fennel.

3 Heat the oil in a wok and stir-fry the pieces of eel for 4 to 5 minutes. Add the ginger, diced parsnips and fennel, together with the fennel seeds and fry for another 3 to 4 minutes. Season with salt and cayenne pepper and pour in the stock. Braise at a moderate temperature for about 6 to 8 minutes.

4 Wash and dry the parsley and pluck the leaves from the stalks. Serve the braised eel sprinkled with parsley and bits of lemon zest.

Sweet and Sour Fish with Onions

1 Peel and dice the shallots. Heat the peanut oil in a wok and fry the diced shallots for 5 to 6 minutes.

2 Add the vinegar, fish stock, bay leaf, spices, chilies, thyme, salt and cook for 6 to 8 minutes at a moderate temperature.

3 Wash the fish fillets, dry and cut into small cubes. Then turn them over in the cornstarch.

4 Put the fish cubes in the stock. Cook at a moderate temperature for about 5 to 6 minutes while stirring. Serve the fish with the onions and the sauce. Goes well with rice.

Serves 4

generous 1 lb/500 g shallots

5–6 tbsp peanut oil

6 tbsp sherry vinegar

1 cup/250 ml fish stock (ready-to-use)

1 crushed bay leaf

clove, mustard and ginger powder

coarse black pepper

1–2 crushed dried chilies

1 tsp thyme flakes

salt

sugar

generous 1 lb/500 g whitefish fillets

2 tsp cornstarch

Preparation time: ca. 25 minutes
342 kcal/1438 kJ

121

Fish Curry with Fresh Bamboo Shoots

1 Clean, wash and chop the spring onions. Clean and wash the bamboo shoots, and cut into 2 in/5 cm pieces. Braise in some oil until almost soft.

2 Wash the kaffir lime leaves and the Thai basil leaves, cut into thin strips and put aside. Clean, wash and halve the chilies, remove the base of the stalk, de-seed and chop.

3 Peel the giant prawns and de-gut. Cut the fish into cubes. Fry the fish cubes, prawns and spring onions in peanut oil in a wok. Take out and keep warm.

4 Bring the coconut cream to the boil, allow to simmer while stirring constantly until the surface has an oily sheen. Stir in the curry paste, coconut milk and bamboo shoots, followed by the fish sauce, sugar, kaffir lime leaves and chilies.

5 Heat the mixture, fold in the fish and the prawns and also warm up. Season the fish curry to taste and serve garnished with Thai basil.

Serves 4

1 bunch spring onions

7 oz/200 g fresh bamboo shoots

peanut oil for frying

4 kaffir lime leaves

1 bunch Thai basil

2 fresh red chilies

8 giant prawns

1 ¼ lb/600 g monkfish fillet (angler fish)

1 cup/225 ml coconut cream

1 ½ tbsp red curry paste

2 cups/500 ml coconut milk

2 tbsp fish sauce

2 tsp sugar

Preparation time: ca. 10 minutes (plus frying time)
158 kcal/664 kJ

123

Deep-Fried Fish Slices

1 Defrost the fish fillets and mince finely, together with the onion-garlic mixture and the herbes de Provence. Dice the bacon and work in.

2 Season the fish mixture with salt, pepper, ginger and mustard powder. Whisk the eggs. Cut the bread into thin slices, cutting into the crust a little on all sides.

3 Brush the bread slices with some egg. Spread some of the fish mixture on top and sprinkle with sesame seeds. Press on firmly and brush with egg again.

4 Heat the oil in a wok. Put the bread slices in a skimming ladle with the fish paste side down and immerse in the oil. Deep-fry at a moderate temperature for about 3 to 4 minutes until crispy.

5 Drain the fish slices on a paper towel. Cut the lemon into eight wedges. Serve the fish slices garnished with the lemon wedges accompanied by some plum sauce in a separate dish.

Serves 4

generous 1 lb/500 g saltwater fish fillets

1 tsp salt

1 tsp pepper

2 tbsp sesame oil

2–3 tbsp rice wine

½ bunch spring onions

1 piece of fresh ginger (¾ –1 in/2–3 cm)

3 tbsp flour

2–3 eggs

¾ cup/100 g white sesame seeds

peanut oil for deep-frying

2 lemons

½ bunch parsley

soy sauce

hoisin sauce

wasabi

sambal oelek

*Preparation time: ca. 35 minutes
(plus marinating time)
398 kcal/1674 kJ*

Fish Chips with Sesame Crust

1   Wash and dry the fish fillets, and then freeze them a little in a freezer. Take out and cut into thin slices. Mix the salt, pepper, oil and rice wine.

2   Clean and wash the spring onions and cut into fine rings. Peel and finely chop the ginger. Add the spring onions and the ginger to the marinade and pour over the fish slices. Allow to marinate for about 10 to 15 minutes.

3   Put the flour on a flat plate. Whisk the eggs, and put the sesame seeds in a dish. Heat sufficient peanut oil in a wok. Take the fish slices out of the marinade and turn over in flour, eggs and sesame seeds, one after the other. Deep-fry the fish chips in portions in hot oil for about 2 to 3 minutes.

4   Remove and drain on a paper towel. Cut the lemons into slices. Wash and dry the parsley and remove the leaves.

5   Garnish the fish chips with lemon slices and parsley. Serve with some soy sauce, hoisin sauce, wasabi and sambal oelek as dips.

Sole with Thai Basil and Kaffir Lime

Serves 4

1 ¼ lb/600 g fillet of sole

14 oz/400 g carrots

2 kaffir limes

1 tbsp oyster sauce

2 tbsp fish sauce

4 tbsp vegetable oil

3 tbsp soy sauce

1 bunch Thai basil

*Preparation time: ca. 15 minutes
(plus 30 minutes marinating time)
285 kcal/1195 kJ*

1   Wash the sole, dab dry and cut into strips of 1 ¼ in/ 3 cm. Wash, clean and peel the carrots, halve lengthways and diagonally cut into thin slices. Cut the kaffir limes into thin slices.

2   Marinate the pieces of sole in oyster and fish sauce for 30 minutes.

3   Heat the oil in a wok and slowly cook the carrot slices until soft. Add the kaffir lime slices and the fish pieces, stir and fry for about 2 minutes. Pour in the soy sauce and stir in the Thai basil leaves.

126

Sweet and Sour Gilthead with Leek and Carrot Strips

Serves 4

**4 gilthead fillets with skin
(4 ¼ oz/120 g each)**

6 medium size carrots

4 leeks

4 tbsp vegetable oil

2 tbsp tomato ketchup

4 tbsp sweet & sour sauce

2 tbsp fish sauce

2 sprigs coriander

*Preparation time: ca. 25 minutes
347 kcal/1455 kJ*

1   Wash the fish filets, dab them dry and remove the bones. Cut into 1 in/3 cm long pieces. Wash and peel the carrots, cut into strips with a peeler. Cut the leeks into strips of about 6 in/15 cm, wash and shake dry.

2   Sear the fish pieces in 2 tablespoons of hot oil in a wok on the skin side only and remove.

3   Fry the vegetables at a high temperature in the remaining oil, allow to collapse and season with ketchup and sweet and sour sauce. Pour in the fish sauce. Add the fish pieces and mix carefully. Finally stir in the finely chopped coriander.

Scorpion Fish with Fried Broccoli and Ginger

1 Wash the fish filets, dab them dry and cut into ¾ in/ 2 cm wide strips. Cut the chilies into rings. Marinate the fish and the chilies in the fish sauce for about 1 hour.

2 Cut the lemon grass into pieces of about 2 in/5 cm. Cut the leek into rings. Wash the broccoli, divide into small segments, peel the stalk and cut into pieces.

3 Heat half of the peanut oil in a wok and gently fry the broccoli florets and pieces with the lemon grass. Add the leek rings and pour in the oyster sauce. Finally add the grated ginger and mix. Take out and keep warm.

4 Heat the remaining peanut oil in the wok and add the fish pieces. Fry gently from all sides for 5 minutes at a moderate temperature.

5 Serve the broccoli and the leek with the fried fish fillet pieces.

Serves 4

4 scorpion fish fillets with skin

2 tbsp fish sauce

2 green chilies

4 stalks lemon grass

1 leek

generous 1 lb/500 g broccoli

4 tbsp peanut oil

4 tbsp oyster sauce

1 tbsp grated ginger

Preparation time: ca. 20 minutes (plus 1 hour marinating time)
388 kcal/1634 kJ

127

9 oz/250 g lotus roots

9 oz/250 g cucumber

9 oz/250 g carrots

7 tbsp/100 ml cider vinegar

1 cup/250 ml vegetable stock (ready-to-use)

2–3 tsp sugar

½ tsp salt

8 bamboo leaves

generous 1 lb/500 g sea bass fillets

2–3 tbsp sesame oil

2–3 tbsp ginger juice

2–3 tbsp rice wine

9 oz/250 g mussels in a jar

Preparation time: ca. 40 minutes
406 kcal/1706 kJ

Steamed Bass

1   Peel the lotus roots and make cuts into the areas between the cavities. Then cut into thin rings. Peel the cucumber and carrots and cut into thin slices.

2   Mix the cider vinegar with the vegetable stock and the spices. Bring the mixture to the boil in a wok. Add the vegetables prepared earlier and cook at a low temperature for about 5 to 6 minutes. Then remove and allow to drain well.

3   Rinse the bamboo leaves with warm water and allow to dry. Put the bamboo leaves in a steamer basket letting them stick out over the edges enough to use them to cover the food to be steamed later.

4   Wash and dry the bass fillets. Mix the oil with the ginger juice and the rice wine and marinate the fish fillets in this mixture for 4 to 5 minutes. Put the mussels in a strainer and allow to drain well.

5   Spread the mixed vegetables on the bamboo leaves. Put the fish fillets with the marinade on top, followed by the mussels. Fold the bamboo leaves to enclose the food and then place the packages in the steamer basket.

6   Bring the vegetable stock to the boil again and put the steamer basket in the wok. Steam at a low temperature for about 10 minutes covered with a lid.

Serves 4

1 bunch spring onions

3–4 garlic cloves

3–4 chilies

1 ¾ lb/800 g saltwater fish fillets

salt

pepper

1 tbsp dried lemon grass flakes

1 tbsp ginger powder

1 tsp turmeric

4–5 tbsp peanut oil

1 ½ cups/350 ml coconut milk, unsweetened

1 tbsp coconut cream

1 tbsp chili sauce (ready-to-use)

Preparation time: ca. 30 minutes
855 kcal/3592 kJ

Special Fish Balls with Sweet and Sour Sauce

1 Clean, wash, dry and chop the spring onions. Peel the garlic cloves. Halve the chilies, de-seed and wash under cold running water.

2 Wash the fish fillets, dry and cut into pieces. Finely mince the fish, together with the spring onions, garlic cloves and chilies. Season the fish mixture with the spices and form into small balls.

3 Heat the oil in a wok and fry the fish balls for about 5 to 6 minutes in batches. Take out and keep warm.

4 Stir the coconut milk together with the coconut cream and the chili sauce into the oil left from frying. Add the fish balls and cook for about 10 minutes at a low temperature. Serve the fish balls with the sauce.

Halibut with Mixed Sprouts

1 Clean, wash and dry the halibut and cut into thin strips. Sprinkle the fish strips with lemon juice and season with salt and pepper.

2 Heat the oil in a wok and fry the fish strips for about 4 minutes in portions. Put the kidney beans in a strainer and allow to drain well. Rinse the sprouts with cold water and also allow to drain well.

3 Add the beans and the sprouts to the fish strips and stir-fry for about 3 to 4 minutes. Season with soy sauce.

4 Roast the nori sheets on one side in a pan without any oil and then crumble them. Serve the halibut sprinkled with the crumbled nori sheets and garnished with lemon.

Serves 4

1 ¾ lb/800 g halibut

lemon juice for sprinkling

salt

pepper

5–6 tbsp sesame oil

¾ cup/200 g kidney beans, canned

generous 1 lb/500 g mixed sprouts (ready-to-use)

2–3 tbsp soy sauce

2–3 nori (seaweed) sheets

lemon wedges for garnishing

Preparation time: ca. 25 minutes
482 kcal/2024 kJ

Seafood

Some of the world's best seafood recipes come from Asia. They are easy to cook and bring the exotic taste of the Far East to your table with relatively little effort. Discover the culinary diversity of mussels, prawns, crayfish, and squid, prime ingredients enhanced with tasty marinades or deep-fried and crispy.

134

Crayfish Curry

1   Wash the crayfish under running water and detach the claws. Twist off the heads.

2   Peel and dice the shallots. Peel the garlic cloves and chop finely. Wash the chilichilies, halve lengthwise, remove the seeds and cut into strips.

3   Heat the sunflower oil in a wok and fry the shallots with the garlic and the chilichilies. Add the crayfish pieces and sprinkle with curry powder.

4   Clean, wash, and chop the spring onions and also add. Pour in the fish and soy sauce, rice wine vinegar and lime juice after about 2 minutes.

5   Peel the kaffir lime, finely chop the peel and stir in with the palm sugar. After about 6 minutes, serve in small bowls garnished with coriander.

Serves 4

2–2 ¼ lb/900 g–1 kg giant prawns, headless, raw in the shell

sesame oil for deep-frying

10 garlic cloves

3–4 red chilies

1 bunch spring onions

lemon-pepper seasoning

3 ½ oz/100 g sweet & sour pickled ginger

2 tbsp peanut oil

lime for garnishing

Preparation time: ca. 35 minutes
499 kcal/2097 kJ

Special Garlic Prawns

1   Wash and dry the giant prawns and deep-fry for about 40 to 50 seconds in very hot sesame oil until red. Take out and drain on a paper towel.

2   Peel and finely chop the garlic cloves. Halve and de-seed the chilichilies and wash under cold running water. Cut into fine rings.

3   Clean and wash the spring onions, cut into rings and mix with the diced chilies and the garlic cloves. Season with the lemon-pepper seasoning.

4   Finely chop the ginger and add to the onion-garlic mixture. Heat the peanut oil in a wok and stir-fry the mixed vegetables for about 3 to 4 minutes.

5   Add the giant prawns and stir for 1 to 2 minutes. Serve garnished with lime.

Prawns Maharaja

1   Gut, wash and dry the prawns, add 4 peeled and pressed garlic cloves. Mix with ginger, tamarind, turmeric, sugar, 1 teaspoon of salt and some chili powder. Allow to stand for 10 minutes.

2   Clean, halve, wash, de-seed and chop the chilichilies.

3   Stir-fry 5 peeled and crushed garlic cloves in oil until golden brown. Add the prawn mixture and stir-fry for 1 minute.

4   Add the coconut milk and the chilichilies in the wok. Heat up, season with salt and serve hot.

Serves 4

1 ¾ lb/800 g shelled prawns

9 garlic cloves

1 piece ginger, freshly grated

4 tsp tamarind paste

½ tsp turmeric

½ tsp sugar

salt

chili powder

vegetable oil

2 fresh green chilies

1 ½ cups/350 ml coconut milk

Preparation time: ca. 20 minutes (plus standing time)
250 kcal/1050 kJ

137

Mussels with Lemon Grass and Basil

1 Clean the mussels by brushing them and removing the beard. Discard any open mussels.

2 Cook the mussels in water for 10 minutes, drain and take out of the shell. Remove any mussels that have not opened.

3 Peel and chop the onions and garlic. Chop the lemon grass. Halve, de-seed, wash and finely chop the chilies.

4 Heat the oil in a wok. Add the onion, garlic, lemon grass and chili. Stir-fry at a medium temperature for about 5 minutes.

5 Add the wine and fish sauce and cook for 3 minutes. Add the mussels, stir well and cook for another 3 to 5 minutes at a low temperature with the lid on.

6 Sprinkle with Thai basil and serve with steamed rice.

Serves 4

2 ¼ lb/1 kg small ommon mussels

1 onion

4 garlic cloves

2 stalks lemon grass

1–2 tsp red chilies

1 tbsp oil

1 cup/250 ml white wine

1 tbsp fish sauce

16 Thai basil leaves

Preparation time: ca. 40 minutes (plus soaking time)
199 kcal/836 kJ

139

Fried Seafood

Serves 4

1 ¾ lb/800 g seafood
(frozen)

1–2 tbsp five-spice powder

1 sprig rosemary

½ bunch thyme

1 tbsp lemon juice

1 tbsp capers

3 tbsp/20 g pitted black olives

7 oz/200 g dried tomatoes in oil

4–5 tbsp peanut oil

4 tsp grappa

chopped chives for garnishing

Preparation time: ca. 25 minutes
409 kcal/1720 kJ

1   Defrost the seafood according to the instructions on the package. Sprinkle with the five-spice powder and allow to stand for about 5 minutes.

2   Wash and dry the herbs, pluck off the leaves and chop finely. Mix the herbs with the lemon juice and the well-drained capers. Chop the olives and add.

3   Put the tomatoes in a strainer and drain well. Then chop coarsely and also add to the mixed herbs.

4   Heat the oil in a wok and stir-fry the seafood for 3 to 4 minutes. Remove and keep warm.

5   Fry the herb-olive-tomato mixture in the oil left from frying for about 3 to 4 minutes. Add the seafood again and heat for 1 minute. Season to taste with grappa, serve sprinkled with chives.

Giant Prawns in Rice Wine

1 Rinse the giant prawns thoroughly under running water, dry well and marinate in rice wine for 30 minutes.

2 Heat the oil in a wok, dissolve the ground palm sugar in the oil, stir in the oyster sauce, add the chili flakes and fry the giant prawns from all sides at a high temperature.

3 Pour the marinade over the prawns, cover the wok with a lid and cook the giant prawns for about 3 to 5 minutes. Remove the giant prawns from the wok and serve sprinkled with the sauce.

Serves 4

20 large giant prawns in the shell with heads

generous ¾ cup/200 ml rice wine

6 tbsp vegetable oil

1 tsp palm sugar

4 tbsp oyster sauce

1 tsp chili flakes

Preparation time: ca. 15 minutes (plus 30 minutes marinating time) 305 kcal/1276 kJ

Fried Scallops

1 Wash and dry the scallops thoroughly and marinate with lemon peel and sesame oil for 10 minutes.

2 Wash, clean and diagonally cut the spring onions into lengths of 1 ½ in/4 cm. Skin, quarter and de-seed the tomatoes and cut into wedges. Finely chop the peeled garlic and de-seeded chili.

3 Fry the spring onions in a wok using half of the oil, add the tomatoes, ginger, garlic and chili and concanue to fry for another 3 minutes. Season to taste with oyster and fish sauce. Take out.

4 Heat the remaining oil in the wok and fry the scallops until golden. Serve on plates with the spring onions.

Serves 4

12 scallops without shells and roe

1 pinch of grated lemon peel

1 tbsp roasted sesame oil

1 bunch spring onions

7 oz/200 g tomatoes

1 garlic clove

1 red chili

4 tbsp sunflower oil

1 tsp freshly grated ginger

2 tbsp oyster sauce

2 tbsp fish sauce

Preparation time: ca. 35 minutes (plus 10 minutes marinating time) 142 kcal/593 kJ

Deep-fried Prawn Balls

Serves 4

9 oz/250 g raw prawns

1 ½ oz/40 g dried rice vermicelli

1 egg

1 tbsp fish sauce (ready-to-use)

⅔ cup/100 g flour

3 spring onions

1 red chili

½ teaspoon bagoong

oil for deep-frying

Preparation time: ca. 20 minutes (plus deep-frying time)
186 kcal/780 kJ

1 Peel and gut the prawns, then wash and drain them. Purée half of the prawns in a food processor. Chop the rest of the prawns into small pieces and mix well with the puréed prawns.

2 Put the vermicelli in a bowl and cover with hot water. Allow to soak for 1 minute. Remove the water and cut the vermicelli into short pieces.

3 Whisk the egg with about ¾ cup/150 ml of water and the fish sauce. Put the flour in a bowl, make an indentation in the center, slowly add the egg mixture and stir until a smooth dough is obtained.

4 Clean, wash and chop the spring onions. Clean, wash and halve the chilichili, remove the base of the stalk, de-seed and chop. Add the prawn mixture, bagoong (shrimp paste), spring onions, chili and vermicelli and mix.

5 Heat the oil to a high temperature. Place tablespoon-sized portions of the prawn mixture in the oil and deep-fry for 3 minutes, until the balls are crispy and golden brown. Remove and allow to drain on a paper towel.

Tiger Prawns

Serves 4

½ cup/125 ml lobster stock

4 tbsp fermented black beans

1 ¾ lb/750 g raw tiger prawns in the shell

7 tbsp oyster sauce

2 tbsp fish sauce

2 dried anchovies

5 tbsp light soy sauce

2 tbsp chili sauce

11 oz/300 g shiitake mushrooms

2 red-yellow habaneros

11 oz/300 g yard-long beans

1 bitter cucumber

5 tbsp sesame oil

2 tbsp red curry paste

3 tbsp coconut cream

salt

pepper

4 tbsp peanut oil

3 tbsp sesame seeds

Preparation time: ca. 20 minutes (plus 30 minutes each marinating and soaking time)
531 kcal/2231 kJ

1   Heat the lobster stock and soak the beans for about 30 minutes in this liquid. Wash and dry the prawns. Mix the oyster sauce with the fish sauce and stir in the crumbled anchovies. Add the soy sauce and the chili sauce and stir. Marinate the prawns in this mixture for about 30 minutes.

2   Clean, wash and chop the mushrooms. Wash the habanero chilies, halve lengthwise, remove the seeds and cut into pieces. Clean, wash and chop the yard-long beans. Clean, wash and slice the bitter cucumber.

3   Heat the sesame oil and braise the vegetables. Stir in the curry paste and the coconut cream. Season with salt and pepper.

4   Heat the peanut oil in a wok and fry the prawns for about 4 minutes. Add the sesame seeds. Serve the prawns with the vegetables on plates.

Calamari with Mixed Vegetables

1 Partially defrost the mixed stir-fry vegetables. Put the water chestnuts, bamboo shoots and palm hearts in a strainer and allow to drain well. Cut everything into fine slices.

2 Heat the oil in a wok and stir-fry all of the vegetables for about 4 to 5 minutes. Season to taste with the spices, salt and pepper.

3 Wash, dry and add the calamari and stir-fry for another 3 to 4 minutes. Wash and dry the coriander and remove the leaves.

4 Serve the calamari on plates, sprinkled with coriander leaves.

Serves 4

generous 1 lb/500 g Chinese stir-fry vegetables (frozen)

3 ½ oz/100 g water chestnuts, canned

3 ½ oz/100 g bamboo shoots, canned

3 ½ oz/100 g palm hearts, canned

6–7 tbsp sesame oil

ginger, garlic and onion powder

salt

pepper

generous 1 lb/500 g calamari (baby squid)

½ bunch coriander

Preparation time: ca. 30 minutes
304 kcal/1276 kJ

Crispy Prawns

1 Peel the prawns and gut. Put the heads and shells in a pot of water. Clean, wash and chop the spring onions and add. Bring to the boil and allow to simmer for 15 minutes. Strain, catching ½ cup/125 ml of the liquid and put aside.

2 Stir the prawns thoroughly with 1 teaspoon of salt for 1 minute and then rinse with cold water. Repeat this procedure twice, using ½ a teaspoon of salt each time. Finally rinse well and dry. Mix 1 tablespoon of cornstarch with the beaten egg white, and allow the prawns to marinate in the mixture for 30 minutes, covered with a lid.

3 Wash the peas. Clean, wash and halve the pepper. Remove the base of the stalk and the seeds and cut the pepper into thin strips.

4 For the sauce, mix the prawn liquid with the oyster sauce, rice wine, remaining cornstarch and sesame oil.

5 Heat the oil, deep-fry the prawns for 1 to 2 minutes and take out. Allow to drain on a paper towel and keep warm.

6 Remove the oil leaving only about 2 tablespoons. Peel, press and add the garlic, add the ginger and stir-fry for 30 seconds. Stir-fry the peas and pepper pieces for 2 minutes. Stir in the prepared sauce seasoning mixture and heat up. Finally carefully add the prawns and serve.

Serves 4

1 ¼ lb/600 g prawns

4 spring onions

2 tsp salt

1 ½ tbsp cornstarch

1 egg white

generous ¾ cup/125 g snow peas

1 small red pepper

1 tbsp oyster sauce

1 tbsp rice wine

1 tsp sesame oil

oil for deep-frying

½ tsp garlic

½ tsp grated fresh ginger

Preparation time: ca. 25 minutes (plus 30 minutes marinating time)
202 kcal/848 kJ

147

Crayfish with Artichokes

Serves 4

2 ¼ lb–3 ¼ lb/1–1 ½ kg crayfish (frozen, boiled in the shell)

2 garlic cloves

4 shallots

coriander, cumin, and ginger powder

1 tbsp chili sauce

4–5 tbsp sesame oil

11 oz–14 oz/300–400 g artichoke hearts, canned

½ cup/125 ml Asian-style stock (ready-to-use)

cornstarch

cucumber slices for serving

Preparation time: ca. 30 minutes
427 kcal/1793 kJ

1 Defrost the crayfish according to the directions on the package. Pull off and cut open the tails and remove the meat. Cut the crayfish meat into pieces.

2 Peel and dice the garlic cloves and shallots. Mix with the crayfish meat and season to taste with the spices and the chili sauce.

3 Heat the oil in a wok and stir-fry the crayfish mixture for 3 to 4 minutes.

4 Put the artichoke hearts in a strainer and drain well. Cut the hearts into small cubes and put in the wok together with the Asian-style stock. Braise together with the crayfish mixture at a moderate temperature for about 1 to 2 minutes.

5 Mix the cornstarch with some cold water and use to thicken the crayfish-artichoke mixture. Serve the crayfish with the artichokes on a bed of cucumber slices.

148

Special Scallops with Tomatoes

1 Clean, wash, dry and cut the spring onions into fine rings. Peel and finely chop the garlic cloves. Cut the skin of the tomatoes crosswise, quickly dip into boiling water, rinse with cold water and skin. Cut into small cubes.

2 Heat the oil in a wok and stir-fry the spring onions with the garlic and the tomato cubes for 2 to 3 minutes. Season with salt, pepper and a pinch of sugar.

3 Wash, dry and halve the mussels. Put the mushrooms in a strainer and allow to drain well. Then cut in half.

4 Add the mussels and the mushrooms to the vegetables and stir-fry for 1 minute. Add the sherry and the soy sauce, heat up and season to taste with salt and pepper if necessary. Serve the scallops garnished with lemon slices.

Serves 4

1 bunch spring onions

2 garlic cloves

3 beef tomatoes

4–5 tbsp sesame oil

salt

pepper

sugar

generous 1 lb/500 g scallops without shells

3 ½ oz/100 g button mushrooms, canned

4 tsp/20 ml sherry

1 tbsp soy sauce

1 lemon

Preparation time: ca. 20 minutes
468 kcal/1966 kJ

Desserts

The sweet finale of an Asian menu can easily be prepared in a wok. The small selection of fruity sweets presented in this section includes delicacies such as steamed fruit wontons, deep-fried pineapples, sweet potato balls and fried bananas.

Serves 4

generous ¾ cup/125 g flour

1 ½ tbsp sugar

½ tbsp clarified butter

1 apple

1 pear

1 tbsp lemon juice

4 peach halves, canned

1 baby pineapple

2–3 tbsp honey

1–2 tbsp cinnamon sugar

2–3 tbsp ground almonds

lemon balm for garnishing

Preparation time: ca. 35 minutes
330 kcal/1389 kJ

Steamed Fruit Wontons

1 Sieve the flour in a bowl. Add ½ tablespoon of sugar. Heat up 3 ½ tbsp/50 ml of water and stir in together with the clarified butter.

2 Knead into a smooth dough. Roll out the dough on a work surface dusted with flour until extremely thin and then cut out 12 equally sized squares.

3 Peel the apple and the pear, remove the seeds and grate finely. Sprinkle with lemon juice straight away. Put the peaches in a strainer, allow to drain well and cut into small cubes. Peel the pineapple, remove the stalk and also cut into small cubes.

4 Mix the honey with the cinnamon sugar and the ground almonds. Add the fruit and then distribute the mixture in the middle of the pastry squares. Twist the four corners together at the top.

5 Put the wontons in a steamer basket. Bring a sufficient quantity of water and the remaining sugar to a boil in a wok. Put the baskets inside and steam at a moderate temperature for about 10 to 12 minutes with the lid on. Serve the wontons on plates, garnished with lemon balm.

Serves 4

4 baby pineapples

2 cinnamon sticks

1 tbsp star aniseed

1 piece of fresh ginger (¾ in/2 cm)

½ cup/125 ml Batida de Coco (coconut liqueur)

½ cup/125 ml mineral water

3 tbsp walnut oil

1 ¼ cups/180 g flour

2 tbsp honey

1 tbsp baking powder

oil for deep-frying

lemon balm and small pineapple pieces for garnishing

Preparation time: ca. 50 minutes (plus 25 minutes cooling and standing time)
646 kcal/2715 kJ

Deep-fried Pineapple

1   Wash and peel the baby pineapples, leaving the green on top. Then cut the fruit into quarters.

2   Grind the cinnamon sticks and the star aniseed in a mortar. Peel and finely chop the ginger and add to the spices. Grind the mixture in the mortar again. Sprinkle the pineapple with the spices and chill for about 15 minutes.

3   In the meantime, put the coconut liqueur, mineral water, walnut oil and flour in a bowl and mix. Stir in the honey and the baking powder and then let the batter rest for about 10 minutes.

4   Dip the pineapple quarters in the batter allowing any excess to drain off. Heat the oil in a wok and deep-fry the pineapples until golden brown. Finally serve the pineapples on plates, garnished with lemon balm and small pineapple pieces.

Serves 4
⅔ cup/100 g rice flour
⅔ cup/150 ml coconut milk
salt
2 ½ tbsp/40 g butter
5 firm bananas
butter for frying

*Preparation time: ca. 10 minutes
(plus frying time)
338 kcal/1418 kJ*

Fried Banana

1 Put the flour and the coconut milk in a bowl with a pinch of salt and mix until smooth. Melt the butter and stir into the batter evenly.

2 Peel the bananas and halve lengthways, then cut in the middle.

3 Froth up some butter in a pan. Coat the banana pieces with the batter one at a time and fry in the hot butter until golden.

Cinnamon Apple Fritters

1 Peel and core the apples, and cut into rings about ¾ in/2 cm thick. Sprinkle with lemon juice immediately. Then sprinkle with cinnamon sugar and allow to stand for 5 to 6 minutes.

2 For the batter, mix the flour with the eggs, the salt and the sesame seeds.

3 Heat up sufficient peanut oil in a wok. Coat the apple rings with the batter and deep-fry in the hot oil in portions.

4 Serve the apple rings with smooth sour cream or maple syrup.

Serves 4

2–3 apples

2–3 tbsp lemon juice

1–2 tbsp cinnamon sugar

6 tbsp wholeflour

2 eggs

1 pinch of salt

1–2 tbsp sesame seeds

peanut oil for deep-frying

10 tbsp/150 g sour cream or 5–6 tbsp maple syrup

Preparation time: ca. 35 minutes
437 kcal/1835 kJ

Sweet Potato and Poppy Seed Balls

1 Put the sweet potatoes in a strainer and allow to drain well. Then squash with a fork.

2 Stir in the poppy seeds, flour and sugar. Whisk the eggs and also add to the sweet potato mixture. Season to taste with the spices and form into small balls.

3 Heat the coconut butter in a wok and deep-fry the balls until golden. Allow to drain on a paper towel and serve dusted with icing sugar.

Serves 4

generous 1 lb/500 g sweet potatoes, canned

3–4 tbsp poppy seeds

1 tbsp wholemeal flour

1–2 tbsp cane sugar

1–2 eggs

ginger, cardamom and clove powder

some drops of vanilla extract

7 tbsp/100 g coconut butter for deep-frying

icing sugar for dusting

Preparation time: ca. 35 minutes
522 kcal/2192 kJ

Banana Chips

Serves 4

scant 1 cup/100 g brown cane sugar

1–2 tsp each of orange and lemon peel extract

½ cup/50 g ground unsalted peanuts

10 bananas

2–3 tbsp lemon juice

7 tbsp/100 g coconut butter for deep-frying

Preparation time: ca. 35 minutes
624 kcal/2620 kJ

1 Mix the sugar with the orange and lemon peel extract and the peanuts. Peel the bananas and slice lengthways. Sprinkle with lemon juice straight away.

2 Heat the coconut butter in a wok. Turn over the banana slices in the sugar mixture and deep-fry in the hot coconut butter in portions.

3 Take out the banana chips and allow to cool off on a grid. Make sure that the chips do not stick together.

158

Coconut Fruit Omelets

1 Remove the base of the stalks of the sharon fruit and pull off the skin. Cut the fruit into cubes.

2 Peel the kiwis and the guavas and cut into small cubes. Mix the fruit with the sugar, the coconut cream and the desiccated coconut.

3 Beat the eggs for 2 to 3 minutes until fluffy and stir in some mineral water.

4 Heat up the butter and fry thin omelets with portions of the batter. Allow the omelets to drain on a paper towel, distribute the fruit on the omelets, fold in and serve.

Serves 4

4 sharon fruit

2 kiwis

2 guavas

2–3 tbsp brown sugar

7 tbsp/100 ml coconut cream

1 cup/100 g desiccated coconut

4–6 eggs

mineral water

2–3 tbsp coconut butter for frying

Preparation time: ca. 30 minutes
404 kcal/1696 kJ